SING A SONG OF SIXPENCE

HAZEL WHEELER

ISIS
LARGE PRINT
Oxford

Copyright © Hazel Wheeler, 1995

First published in Great Britain 1995
by
Alan Sutton Publishing Ltd

Published in Large Print 2005 by ISIS Publishing Ltd,
7 Centremead, Osney Mead, Oxford OX2 0ES
by arrangement with
the Author

British Library Cataloguing in Publication Data
Wheeler, Hazel
    Sing a song of sixpence. – Large print ed.
    (Isis reminiscence series)
    1. Large type books
    2. Yorkshire (England) – History – 20th century
    3. Yorkshire (England) – Social conditions – 20th
    century
    I. Title
    942.8'1'083

ISBN 0–7531–9328–0 (hb)
ISBN 0–7531–9329–9 (pb)

Printed and bound in Great Britain by
T. J. International Ltd., Padstow, Cornwall

To my children, Elizabeth and Caroline. As all children are — "the best in the world!"

Contents

Acknowledgements

Many thanks to those "Children of Yesteryear" who kindly shared their experiences of childhood with me:

Mrs H. Gledhill, Mrs Irene Hill, Mr John Holmes, Mr and Mrs Clifford Webster, Mr S. Pike, Mr and Mrs D. Boothroyd, Mr G. Wilson, Mr and Mrs K. Greenwood, Mr G. Hill, Miss B. Waddington, Mrs P. Bardon, Mr Tony Mellor and Lenora, Mrs J. Toulcher, Mrs J. Sheard and Betty, Mrs E. Riley, Mr B. Halstead and "Alec".

Also to the *Huddersfield Examiner*, Miss E. Chappell, and anyone else who helped in any way, and to Granville, for "Keeping the Home Fires Burning" while these memories were being written.

Introduction

Childhood was a magical never-never land where, if you were lucky, the words of a song of the 1920s came true:

Little world of gladness, where the bluebells grow,
There's no place upon this earth that I treasure so.
There the sun is always shining, there the skies
   are blue,
And in this little world of ours, there is love and
   you.

This song, one of the most successful ballads of 1920, could be bought in Huddersfield from Taylor's music department in Shambles Lane.

The Land of Make Believe also existed in the cinema, where *Broken Blossoms* was showing at the Empire that January of 1920. Huddersfield Amateur Operatic Society's choice was *Gipsy Love* at the Hippodrome.

There was summer-like weather that year up to Good Friday, then it deteriorated. Some things, unlike the calendar, never change. But if one were an optimist,

1

anything could happen — perhaps winning £1, £25, £50 or even £500, and failing that a box of Rowntree's chocolates — by thinking up names for the famous Rowntree Cocoa Nibs — a girl, a boy and a dog. How popular names like Sunny Jim, Pip, Squeak and Wilfred became!

There were fashions peculiar to the 1920s, even in dogs. Airedales were the chums of many a child and there was money to be made if you had a canine partner. One boy became hooked on catching rats when he heard that the council promised to pay ½d a tail. He must have been a workaholic — he caught 200! When most children were given a Saturday ½d or 1d, that must really have boosted his piggy bank.

All was not lost if parents could not afford to take their children away on holiday. Forty children were selected from elementary schools every week during the summer to spend a holiday in the Cinderella Home at Hall Ing, Honley. The public were invited to give 12s 6d to ensure that a child could "have the joy of securing a week's happy holiday, with all its physical and moral benefits". If parents were really quite well off, they may even take their children to see Fred Roper and his Wonderful Midgets in *The Toy Soldier Parade*, a treat in June at Harrogate in 1931.

That other highlight of every child's year, Christmas, could be enlivened, for those who could afford it, with a Children's Dance from 3–5.30p.m. on Christmas Eve afternoon at a cost of 2s each, complete with special dance music, a Christmas tree, and Father Christmas to give each child a present. Other treats might include a visit to the Theatre Royal to see *Babes in the Wood*.

In 1920 Rushworth's, one of the smartest shops in town, had their Toyland on the second floor. Even "just looking" meant a journey into Wonderland. Meccano electric sets cost either 6s, 10s, 20s or up to 180s. How about an electric railway warehouse and lift, signal, lamp and crane, all of which could be put together by any boy with the help of Meccano parts and an electric motor?

Girls were more interested in French jointed dolls, from 4s 11d to 22s 6d, or dolls with closing eyes and real eyelashes, smartly dressed in velvet coat and dainty straw hat for 21s. Chemical Magic Cabinets were priced from 1s 9d to 22s 6d.

Then, for a "big" present, a pedal car, there was the "Victory Motor", pedalled like a cycle, with windscreen and headlamps and costing a mighty £10, though cheaper models were available from 5 guineas. Not surprisingly, most families had to economize prior to toy-buying. But money was of little concern to the children of the 1920s when they saw lovely toys and had the opportunity to enter the Land of Make Believe.

CHAPTER
ONE

Hilda

Augustus Barnett died when his daughter, Hilda, was only four years old. She was then known by some as "Young Gus". At her christening the parson added Margaret to Hilda, because he liked it, which was quite a surprise for her parents!

Hilda was born on 17 April 1908 in West Stockwith on the banks of the River Trent, but was brought up in Greetland with her Grandma and Auntie Alice. Her mother, Rose, re-married, and the child didn't see her again until she was ten. She wouldn't have recognized her mother had she seen her in the street.

The cottage consisted of one room where everything happened — eating, cooking, sleeping. A "shutup" bed against a wall was hauled down at bedtime. There was no kitchen. One nearby dwelling even crammed in a piano, next to the sink!

Always interested in history, Hilda was told about people going down to the river when the tide came in to collect water, as there was no tap water in those early days. There were tub closets, but no one to empty them officially, so householders did it themselves, tossing the contents into the river when the tide was going out, along with other rubbish.

Some people sailed little boats, and when a big wave was imminent a cry went up of "Waar Aegar, Waar Aegar", meaning "Beware, big wave." "Aegar" was the local name for it.

Hilda loved dressing up, and would have loved to have been an actress, but lack of money thwarted her ambitions. But there was a piano at her Grandma's, and Hilda learned to play it. She can't remember a time when she couldn't play the piano, and what joy it brought her. *The Bluebells of Scotland, The Ash Grove* — songs that live forever were the first ones she was taught. She indulged her love of theatre by appearing in local Nativity and Passion plays, and concerts.

Auntie Alice and Grandma fostered the keen intelligence of the little girl who had been entrusted to their care, so much so that Hilda could read perfectly by the time she was four and began lessons in the "Baby Class" at Greetland, where infants stayed until they were seven. Teachers were used to having a lot of children in their classes, as most families had many children, and Hilda remembers the names of one brood — Connie, Ada, Lizzie, Willie, John, Arthur, Jessie, Sylvia and Joan.

Hilda could never understand why there should be separate entrances at school; one for Boys, the other for Girls. Once inside they were in mixed classes and played in the same school yard, so what was the difference?

If they had a bit of land to grow vegetables and fruit bushes people weren't short of wholesome food. Grandma was a keen herbalist. There were bunches of herbs hanging up all over her cottage. Homilies were constantly trotted out, such as "Nothing better than sago pudding for the stomach." She grew enough wormwood to let local mills have some. It was put among the cloth when it had been woven to keep the moths away. If Hilda or anybody else was poorly, Grandma scalded some herb or other for the patient. The remedies were handed down from one generation to another. A doctor was never called in.

There was never time to be bored. Auntie Alice and Grandma had all kinds of fruits bushes: blackberries, blackcurrants, gooseberries, raspberries, elderberry. They made jam, marmalade, wine — "You could make wine out of almost anything — even boot leather I suppose", laughed Hilda. Beer was made to take out to the haymakers. It was as common as having a drink of tea.

Hens were kept, so there were always fresh eggs warm from the nest for Hilda to collect. A couple of pigs were in residence, but during the First World War the government claimed half of every pig, so they took one of theirs.

It was a self-supporting little household. Alice had a sewing machine on which she made all their clothes, and both she and Grandma always had some knitting on the go. It was almost regarded as a sin to sit idle and not have any work on hand. Hilda was taught to knit early on in her life, and adored seeing her work grow, then stitching it together into a garment. Far more interesting that buying a jumper!

Hilda's guardians never failed to give her a birthday party and a superb cake. Lots of school friends were invited. No matter what the actual day of the birthday, the celebration tea was on the nearest Saturday, at four o'clock. The children sat round the table on wooden buffets which were pushed beneath the table when the repast was over. Food was plentiful and varied, with different coloured jellies and a blancmange after the sandwiches.

Presents were mainly home-made and small, but each child was warmly thanked for the pencil, lace-edged handkerchief, or one with a nursery rhyme character on one corner. A little girl gave a peg doll one birthday, made from an ordinary wooden peg, the type gipsies used to hawk round from door to door. The round bit at the top formed the doll's head. A face was painted on, a bit of wool was glued on top for hair, and paper or a bit of cloth made a skirt. Occasionally an India rubber ball or a skipping rope with striped red handles were given as gifts.

Auntie Alice prepared jugs full of delicious lemonade, with thin strips of lemon floating on top. Parents arrived to collect the small guests at seven.

Hilda knew there was a Father Christmas, because she'd seen him when he visited Greetland School. So Grandma hung up one of her long, black, hand-knitted worsted stockings on the high mantelpiece on Christmas Eve. Those stockings were prickly but strong. Next morning the little girl wasn't disappointed.

Inside were an orange and apple, two bright new shiny pennies, a few sweets, a little book, a drawing book, a pencil and chalks.

The turkey which they had for dinner was hand-reared in their own garden, from an egg. Killing it, or one of the hens, was made to look so simple by Grandma. Screw the neck round with a quick twist — that was all there was to it! A quick death. There was rather more to killing a pig. Auntie Alice cut its throat, and Grandma rushed up with a basin to catch the blood, which was made into black pudding, eaten with Colman's mustard and vinegar. Hilda never thought of the killing as something horrible. The animals were treated with kindness and consideration beforehand.

There was a string of wells round the hilly countryside, so a lot of water was drunk. It was free and delicious. Tin baths hanging outside houses were a normal thing to see. At Auntie Alice's there was plenty of hot water in the Yorkshire range boiler. A ladling can (called a laden can) was dipped inside to draw it out.

Hilda's stockings were kept up with elastic garters. An old lady, Miss Wilson, who lived alone in one of the cellar dwellings peculiar to that hilly area, helped eke out a living making them. Hilda remembers sitting on a chair and being told to "put your leg out". Then Miss Wilson made a mark on the length of elastic. It cost 1d or 2d for a new pair of garters.

Hilda only saw her Grandad once. "An old man's head on a pillow, and underneath it some Pomfret cakes" (black Pontefract cakes). He shuffled his hand beneath the pillow, and gave Hilda a couple. Not long after, he died. Though he owned a mill and was well off, Hilda's Grandma didn't get a penny.

When Hilda, aged ten, met her mother, she thought Rose was a fairy princess — especially when she gave her half a crown. She had never had so much in her life before.

But Rose took her daughter with her for a holiday, and kept her until Hilda was fourteen. Though she was treated with kindness, both by her mother and step-father, deep in her heart she longed to return to Greetland to be with her Auntie Alice, who she considered to be her mother in all but name. Hilda kept saying how she wanted to go back "home" so her mother was glad to let her go, and she didn't see her again until she was twenty-one.

How lovely it was to settle down into the busy life with Grandma and Auntie Alice again, even with the outside "closet" and "pittle pots" beneath the beds. To be back where she felt she belonged, with Auntie Alice, who taught her how to make wedding cakes, and decorate them with pretty latticework icing.

When Hilda was a child, Auntie Alice used to coax her naturally curly hair into ringlets, spiralling it round her fingers or tying it up with rags. But when Hilda was ready to begin work the ringlets were cut off.

Many youngsters worked part-time in a mill when they were thirteen, starting at 6a.m. and continuing until midday, and from 6a.m. to 12.30p.m. on Saturdays. Half-timers worked mornings one week, and the afternoons at school, and vice versa on alternate weeks.

Hilda was a Busy Bee from morn till night, exactly how she liked to be. Knitting, sewing — she has never bought a jumper in her life — gardening, acting in plays and concerts, writing letters — then later, preparing articles for magazines, and travelling all over the world.

She has kept a daily dairy since the 1920s. Hilda married William Gledhill and moved to Barkisland. She became secretary of Halifax Authors' Circle, and a great friend of the late Phyllis Bentley, author of many books, including *Inheritance*.

For many years Hilda Gledhill gave talks to various organizations, and still contributes regular local events reportage to the *Huddersfield Examiner*. Never a day goes by without her writing a letter to someone, and never a day passes without her diary being up to date by lunchtime.

The inheritance passed down to her from her Auntie Alice and Grandma — a keen love of nature, writing and self-sufficiency — has proved to be the basis of a far more fulfilling life than any legacy of money could possibly have been.

CHAPTER
TWO

Farmer's Boy

John Holmes, born at Farnley, near Otley 16 December 1917, stood at the top of a steep flight of stairs in his home, Hasling Hall Farm, and gazed down in awe, his first impression of life. That anything could be so enormous. His mother's parents lived in London, and he was only a toddler when taken there for his first visit.

It was a perfect June morning with dew still on the grass, and a pheasant parading flamboyantly through it. Two-year-old John, forgetful of his all-dressed-up-for-the-journey outfit, stumbled after it through the shoulder-high meadow grass. His clothes were wet through, and he had to be changed hurriedly in order to catch the train. There were no buses, and his father had to take them to the station near Harewood by pony and trap.

At the farm John had a wooden horse named Papyrus. He used to hang his seaside bucket, full of hencorn, over its ears then wheel it out to feed the hens.

In 1921 the family moved to Thurstonland, their belongings transported on two Model T Ford flat wagons. Furniture was piled high on one, with sides of bacon and ham that had been cured on the farm, riding on top of the tables and chairs. On the other wagon, held in between more furniture, was a foal, somehow or other secured and probably wondering what on earth was going on. Before long the cover flapped up halfway, revealing the odd sight, and people began pointing and laughing at the cavalcade. Mr Holmes kept getting off to check that everything was all right. The wagons moving so slowly his dad could walk as fast.

Their new home was Manor House Farm. It had a public house alongside, and several children belonging to the pub attended Thurstonland village school. Sarah Love Pontefract was the teacher. She had no children of her own, but behaved in motherly fashion to her small charges. It wasn't long before John was missing. His mother traced him to the infants' school.

"If he wants to come here, let him stay," Mrs Pontefract advised kindly. So he did. The first thing he was told to do was sit at a desk, fold his arms, and go to sleep! The next lesson was more difficult. Teacher had a massive ball of wool, and tried to show the boys how to knit. In the afternoon they were taught dancing, of a kind.

In the classroom was a stove, bounded by a large, all-enveloping fireguard. Stocksmoor children who stayed for dinner, it being too far to walk home and back, usually brought pies which were warmed up on the fireguard by the stove. John was near enough to go home to the farm for dinner.

Infants who "had an accident" after not allowing themselves enough time to leave the room, had to stand near the radiator until their undergarments dried. At least there wasn't much danger of youngsters being knocked down by traffic. In 1923 there were only three cars in Thurstonland: the butcher's van, the parson's motor and Albert Gill's car, which could be converted into a hearse.

The Christmas party at the infants' school was a joyous occasion. For days before, the children made yellow, blue, green and red paper loops, gummed together to make chains and garlands. Mrs Pontefract drawing-pinned them to the walls and hung them from the ceiling. Each child also had a little tin box containing Plasticine to fashion animals and figures from.

How exciting, on Breaking-Up Day, the Friday before the Christmas holiday began, when Mrs Pontefract told the infants to look out of the window. There stood a pony, with twigs fastened to a harness making it resemble a reindeer's antlers, and a red-cloaked, white-whiskered Father Christmas. Then there was a concert, and Florrie White, who had a lovely voice, sang ballads such as *Old Father Thames*, and carols, before the happy children made their way home.

On Christmas Eve, John dangled one of his own grey woollen knee-length socks with red or green stripes round the tops over the downstairs mantelpiece. On Christmas morning it revealed a few little picture books and games, a bag of his favourite Yorkshire Mixtures, a bag of cinders to remind him that he'd sometimes been bad — but was redeemed — and an orange and apple in the stocking toe.

His Auntie Ethel, who worked for a publishing firm in Leeds, never forgot her nephew's birthday, unlike some relatives who tried to get away with giving only one present, "because his birthday is so near Christmas". Besides a Christmas gift, there was always a book from Auntie Ethel — a big *Boy's Own Annual* or *Chatterbox*. It was wonderful to lay on the rug before a blazing fire, reading on a winter holiday.

Spending money was 1*d* a week. John usually bought "pit props" — finger lengths of chocolate covered with coconut — but it annoyed him that the shopkeeper always seemed to fob him off with broken ones. So, to teach him a lesson, next time he delivered potatoes from the farm, John cut one in two. He was always given unbroken pit props following that cautionary act.

Mr Holmes put 1*s* a week into a savings account for his son at the Yorkshire Penny Bank. When his sister Margaret came on the scene it was halved to 6*d* for each. Later the amount was increased to half a crown per week. Any money John had given, or earned, went straight into his bank account. It was only in 1942, when his savings had accumulated to £100, that he drew it out to marry.

It was somewhat galling though, after earning 7*s* 6*d* a year as the organ-blower at Thurstonland Church, for his mother to make him put it back on the offertory plate immediately. The chap who tolled the bell earned

15

7*s* 6*d* as well, then it was going to be reduced to 6*s*, so he didn't go anymore.

Church services were the natural, accepted way of life on Sundays. Church service at 10.30 a.m., back for Sunday school from 2 till 3, then, if his mother was going to the evening service, he had to go with her. But John didn't mind. He loved the old hymns, and inspiring words. Traditional sounds and words that had rallied worshippers, helping them face hardships, war and deprivation since time immemorial.

When a small boy, John lived in London for a couple of years. His mother had been taken ill when visiting her parents, and John was with her. He hated it. "Please Keep Off The Grass" orders on bits of scrubby parkland, the "built-upness and concrete" of the place. How relieved he was to get back to Thurstonland, the farm, and wild open spaces.

He and his chums revelled in playing in Barncliffe Wood. Damming up a stream with sods of earth. Sailing toy boats. Picnics in the wood. Taking a frying pan, bacon and sausages, and a treacle tin to boil water over a wood fire. Building a fireplace from circles of stones. Perfect freedom.

There were no holidays for the farmer, with the animals to attend to every day. But John, as a perk for blowing the organ, was invited to go on the choir trips. One year they went to Bowness in the Lake District.

In 1927 the farm hand said he could manage on his own when a half-day trip to Blackpool was discussed. The train from Brockholes station didn't leave until 11 a.m. and was scheduled to bring trippers back between 9.30 and 10p.m. However, as will happen to all the best-laid plans of mice and men, the train was shunted into a siding on the return journey, and remained there for three or four hours. It was already 4a.m. when they reached Brockholes station again, with the Dawn Chorus in full song. The disgruntled party set off walking to the farm through the woods. It was almost time to milk the cows, let alone go to bed for a rest.

"We're not going to bother with one of them again," remarked the farmer, the understatement of the journey.

But disappointments fade and new ventures beckon. Mr Holmes read about a 1s 6d evening trip to Grange Moor, on one of the charabancs with rubber tyres, open top, and doors for each seat. At the time of the adventure, John was so small, down on a seat between his father and mother with more adults in front and all around, that all he saw of the journey was the tops of telegraph wires. But children travelled free, so there was that about it. Courting couples on the back seats liked the outing all the better if it began to rain, because then the waterproof cover was pulled over, providing more privacy for "canoodling", as they termed it.

There were, of course, lots of animals on and around the farm, but John fancied having a couple of rabbits as pets. He fed them for a week, then lost interest. One day, on his return from school, he went to have a look at them. They weren't there. He wondered what could have happened. Then he remembered he'd had a rabbit pie a week ago.

When only five or six, John was playing with the pub owner's children. The pub was closed, and they were thirsty, so they decided to drain dregs of beer out of the nearly empty glasses, and ended up feeling very odd indeed.

One Christmas John and a friend went mumming (carol singing). They blacked their faces with soot, and John wore a pair of his father's baggy old check trousers. In the public house taproom next to the farm they sang, danced and played their tambourines. One old fellow playfully pulled John's flyhole open. The child swore at him angrily, which had the effect of more clapping and calling for "encore! encore!" At the end of the impromptu entertainment, the tambourines of both boys were filled with coins.

Dressing up was a big part of childhood. John remembers 1928 as the year he became a Mustard Pot and hated it. He was dressed all in yellow with a yellow cardboard spoon sticking out by his head. How daft grown-ups can make children feel!

The Colman's Mustard Club campaign was launched in 1926. In those days the Colman's name and symbol were everywhere, on cartons, packing cases, enamelled street signs and on shop walls. Children were introduced to the brand through cabinets built by Colman's for school classrooms, bearing the donor's name. Schools were supplied with wall charts, and Colman's illustrated booklets of fairy tales, produced as free handouts, were often the only Christmas gifts received by children of the poor. The campaign's copywriters included detective story writer

Dorothy L. Sayers. "Has Father joined the Mustard Club?" asked posters on London buses, and club memberships were issued along with Mustard Club songs, films and games.

At the fancy-dress parade, John's sister Margaret appeared as Little Bo Peep. Whether or not a flock of Manor House Farm sheep accompanied her has been forgotten. Competitors had to line up in front of the Vicarage to be judged. After all that, John failed to win a prize. But the parson *swore* — and got a prize.

The farmer's boy had an obsession with the family phonograph at one time, especially with a recording of *Whistling Rufus*. He played it not once, not twice, but over and over again, for weeks and weeks, until his mother grabbed a hammer and ruined it.

Another obsession of his 1920s childhood was with Sunny Jim, the lively looking character on packets of Force, the first ready-to-eat flaked breakfast cereal in Britain, introduced from Canada in 1902 at 7½d a packet, and subsequently promoted by the ebullient figure in monocle and Regency clothes. The first advertising jingle proclaimed:

> Jim Dumps was a most unfriendly man,
> Who lived his life on the hermit plan.
> In his gloomy way he'd gone through life
> And made the most of woe and strife,
> Till Force one day was served to him.
> Since then they've called him Sunny Jim.

But the best-known slogan was:

High o'er the fence leaps Sunny Jim,
Force is the food that raises him.

A common joke was:

"I can't coax my husband to eat any breakfast."
"Have you tried Force?"
"Madam, you don't know my husband!"

When household tasks were completed, and boots cleaned and stacked in a row behind a curtain, then it was time for play. Making cardboard houses and stuff like that, using any scraps that happened to be lying about. Matchboxes, with cardboard wheels made from cutting round a big penny or half a crown, with matchsticks pushed into them for pulling, made ideal little carts for a pretend farmyard, complete with Plasticine bulls and cows.

When John possessed a Meccano set, the crane was used to crane the cats up. The farm cats, Kathleen and René, were willing participants in the game. Squeezed into a boot or shoe, the crane hauled them up and down again one at a time. Indeed, they enjoyed it so much they queued up for it!

In 1921 there was one of the harshest frosts in memory. The majority of people had no water toilets, and cold in the bedrooms was so intense that the contents of chamber pots completely froze, as did newly formed manure from the cows. And what a lot of heating it took to warm up only one bedroom in Manor House Farm, a room so large it took twenty rolls of wallpaper to decorate it, and six double beds and one single could easily be accommodated. Earthenware stone hot-water bottles didn't make much of an impression in Arctic conditions such as those in 1921.

When John was fourteen, in 1932, having been to Kaye's College, he left to work on his father's farm. Goodbye to school dinners of sausage and mash for 5d, with a 1d cup of tea, or meat and potato pie at 6d. From then on it was early rising at 5.30a.m., seven days a week, bank holidays included. There were sixteen cows, all to milk by hand. One day he was ploughing a field and saw a familiar figure striding towards him. "Why have we not seen you at Sunday school lately, John?" the parson wanted to know. That did not need a lot of answering.

In the 1920s there were twenty-seven farms in Stocksmoor and Thurstonland. One sow belonging to Manor House Farm had 156 piglets during her life, and ended by being killed, dry-salted in the cellar and hung up in the farm living room to dry over the fire. "It was a very good sow — and made good bacon too," says John.

A decent breakfast of bacon and eggs wasn't eaten until the cows had been milked and other essential work done. Food was better enjoyed after a spot of hard work.

The 1933 winter was another of heavy snowfalls and deep drifts. Starting one Sunday, snow fell for three days and nights without stopping once. Farmer Holmes had to get milk to Stocksmoor Station. He set off with a horse and cart and shovel, got so far and could go no further. The milk was brought back and made into cheese. A man from Shropshire had been fitting individual water bowls in the mistal. The snowdrifts were by then so deep that the man had to stay at the farm for a week before he could attempt to return home.

The Council urged men to bring their own shovels, and shovel snow from the roads, at ½d an hour. Some began at Thurstonland, shovelling towards Stocksmoor. Others began at Thurstonland and continued to Brockholes, probably feeling warmer than they had done for days.

After a visit to London John brought a parrot back to the farm, called (what else?) Pretty Polly. What with *Whistling Rufus* and "Pretty Polly" being repeated over and over again, the noise must have been horrendous. Polly had her one fly-round of the week on Sunday mornings. She escaped once, and the next day a host of starlings flew terrified from out of some trees. Pretty Polly was caught by a local man who put on leather gauntlet gloves, climbed a tree, and brought the parrot down and back to the fold.

John had a few lessons in organ playing from Brian Holmes — no relation — who used to turn up at the farm on his motorbike. From 1921 to around 1925, farm labourers earned 28s a week, so not many youngsters could afford music lessons.

A big bonfire was made to celebrate the Jubilee of King George V and Queen Mary in 1935. It had been arranged to present Albert Gill with a walking stick on that occasion, Albert being the one selected to set the bonfire alight.

Alas, "all the puff" went out of his sails when someone came flying up to say, "Too late, Albert, somebody's set it aleet!" That someone had also taken down the flag and put an old lavatory seat on top. Albert's momentous day had fallen completely flat.

Two years later, in 1937, there was another occasion for a big bonfire at Thurstonland, the Coronation of King George VI and Queen Elizabeth. The huge pile was composed mainly of railway sleepers from Stocksmoor. Pride of place on top was Bert Reddick. Others included Jimmy Jenkinson, Norman Gill, Andrew Pinder, Hugh Smith, William Turner, Matthew Lockwood, Jim Moorhouse and Albert Gill. Amy Thewlis and Hilda Pollard also attended the Coronation celebration bonfire.

In between national celebrations such as the Jubilee and Coronation, there were bonfires galore on 5 November. Little Demons cost 1d, as did Thunderflash Bangers. John and his pals weren't interested in "cissy Fairy Snows and Sparklers". More in their line was putting a banger — already lit — in a treacle tin, quickly putting the lid on, running away fast, then seeing the lot fly up in the air with a blood-curdling bang. John had a swollen hand for a week after some prank or other, "but you didn't bother — you'd had a good time".

Girls were well advised to stay indoors on Bonfire Night. One trick was to tie a length of cotton on a

Jumping Jack, and attack it to the back of a girl's coat. As she ran hysterically away, the Jumping Jack followed.

John tried smoking when young, at a bonfire party. He put the docked-out Woodbine in his coat pocket, forgot about it and put a piece of parkin with it in his pocket. What a horrible taste!

CHAPTER
THREE

Clifford

Clifford Webster, born in 1912, went to the same school as Mary Tinker, Newmill Church School. His father was first a miner, then went into textiles. Clifford had an older sister, Edna. When a child, he had diphtheria, and was taken to isolation hospital in a horse-drawn ambulance.

As a boy in the twenties he collected newspapers from Thongsbridge Station after school and delivered them on his bike round Totties, Wooldale and Scholes. On Saturday mornings Bert Mallinson went with him. Bert's father had bought him a lock-up wooden hut when he became sixteen. Part of the hut was used for selling newspapers, razor blades and odds and ends and the other half as a barber's shop. Bert employed Clifford both to deliver papers and as a "lather boy", as well as to wind up the wooden chair when customers were ready to lean back for a shave. Clifford had to keep the water topped up and boiling on the gas ring. Bert was the only one allowed to use the cut-throat razors.

Bert paid his friend and workmate 6s a week. A haircut cost 5d, a shave 3d.

Old men customers of the barber's shop regularly quoted poems or other ancient saws learned in their schooldays. Without fail, one particular elderly gent came out with one as soon as his head was prostrate on the wooden chair. Clifford knew word for word what he'd say: "Easter Sunday is the first Sunday after the first full moon after 21 March."

In idle moments between customers, the lads used to have wrestling bouts. One disastrous Saturday morning, after the paper round was finished and the shop opened about half past eight, the pair were "acting the goat" when the pan of boiling water was bumped into and the contents poured down the back of Clifford's legs. Doctor Trotter was called upon to dress them. A big blister had formed, and the skin was peeling off. Clifford howled in agony. Doctor Trotter paused, and gazed up at him with a look of amazement in his eyes. "You soft bugger," was all he said. And Clifford immediately calmed down. No boy wants to be known as a coward, even though he is suffering the pangs of Hell!

Clifford had had an earlier encounter with Doctor Trotter when he was only seven or eight. The boy loved haymaking time, and was only too happy to be allowed to help on farms for nothing, simply for the pleasure of the Great Outdoors, the clean, fresh smell of the hay, and the camaraderie of the fields.

He got more than he bargained for, though, when he tried to scratch wheat out of the cogs of a hay-chopper. A finger on his left hand became caught. Doctor Trotter had to pull the nail off, and the scars remained throughout his life. More injuries seemed to be caused by sheer accident and "playing around" than any other way. Curiosity was often a cause as well. The "What will happen if I do this?" kind of thing.

When Clifford was fourteen he began working full time for Wallaces, the grocers, delivering orders and other jobs. He earned 9s for the full week.

Happy times were spent playing tenor horn with Hepworth Band, joining when he was fourteen. One of the pieces they played was called *The Village Wedding*.

Clifford attended Lydgate Sunday school. So did Mary Tinker. Clifford Webster liked the look of young Mary Tinker from Eastfield Farm. He liked the way she had plenty to talk about too. They married, a village wedding, and still live in harmony at Croft Bottom Cottage, New Mill, a picturesque, rural idyll where Mary has only the birds to compete with.

CHAPTER
FOUR

Mary

Mary Tinker was the last of nine children, born at Eastfield Farm near New Mill in 1915. Willie, her father, was a tailor by trade. His wife helped run the smallholding. Willie had a board which was placed on the kitchen table to work on. He made threepiece suits for men at 50s, ladies' costumes, and his family's coats as well, if there was time. Mary did have a cheap fur muff bought once when she was a child. Otherwise it was hand-me-downs.

Her father walked as far as Derbyshire with cloth samples and to take customers' measurements. Willie liked a drop to drink and wasn't the slightest bit concerned if he missed the last train back from Wortley. He was never frightened of anything and could walk 20 miles a day "on a piece of cheese and a raw onion".

It was a Spartan life. Mrs Tinker used to wash, bake, and go to Park Mill Colliery to fetch coal. It was cheaper if a customer collected it than having it delivered. She went by horse and cart, but Sally, the horse, was long in the tooth and almost on her knees. Mary, even as a child, wasn't averse to using a few expletives. When Sally rolled over, fagged out, Mary yelled, "There'll be Hell to pop!"

Birthdays came and went without so much as a greetings card, and there wasn't much point in hanging a stocking up on Christmas Eve. The only thing that may be in it was a hole.

In one of the cold, spacious upstairs rooms were three iron bedsteads and a bedroom suite. The children shared the beds, trying to sleep some at the top end, others at the opposite end. Mary and her sister Winnie doubled up in a bed on the big landing. On freezing winter nights oven plates were wrapped in old bits of blanket and taken to bed to try and warm the children up a bit.

Lighting was by paraffin lamp, and more than once the bustling, talkative little Mary knocked one over — more "Hell to pop!" But even when the lamps were lit, the child didn't see much of the world. She was eleven before she even went to Huddersfield, the nearest town.

However, there are few lives that do not have some brightness in them, some person or animal that makes life worth living. On the farm there was Shep, a sheepdog. Also, as in the nursery rhyme, Mary had a little lamb, which she named Frisk. It became as attached to her as she was to it. Frisk went shopping with her, to the house that sold sweets. When Mary called, it galloped up to her. Frisk even used to run upstairs to "fancy itself in't glass".

When it was born she fed it with a bottle, and the pair became inseparable. She talked a lot to Frisk, as she did to everybody. Mary chattered away almost non-stop, but sometimes used to think that if you talked a lot you didn't live as long. When she voiced her concern to one of her father's friends the farmer replied, "Well, Mary, tha should have been off long since if that was right."

One day, fed up of the incessant chatter, Willie asked someone if he'd like a parrot. He had one, and said "tha can have it for ten bob". The "parrot" was Mary.

When Mary was only three, her mother and brothers decided to walk to Harden Moss Sheepdog Trials, walking seven miles there and seven back. Mary kept asking, "Aren't we there yet?" and for once her conversation remained on the same topic over and over again. When they reached their destination, after what must have felt to be an eternity, she was too small to see anything above the heads of the spectators.

When the babies had "wind", Mary's mother poured hot water onto caraway seeds, and sprinkled on sugar. A hot cinder in water for cinder tea often did the trick as well. Mustard plasters were for bronchitis, as was Vick spread on brown paper with lard and a sprinkling of nutmeg.

If an illness appeared to be serious, beyond the curative capabilities of Mrs Tinker, Willie strode off at a brisk pace over the fields to summon Dr Kennedy from Shepley. In 1926, Mary was very ill with scarlet fever, and an ambulance arrived at Eastfield Farm to take her to Meltham Isolation Hospital. Poor little Frisk tried to scramble into the ambulance with her.

Patients were wakened at six in the morning. Girls were in one ward, and the boys in another. One medicine — to keep the bowels moving — was liquorice powder in an enamel mug, with water poured onto it. Mary liked Nurse Greenwood and Nurse Webster, who wore white uniforms with mauve pinafores, but there was such sadness when she eventually returned home because her pet, her adored little lamb, Frisk, had been sent to market.

On 24 September 1935 there was a violent thunderstorm. Stewing meat was in the oven, and Mary was seated on the "long saddle seat" near the window mending her corsets. Suddenly, her brother, Clarence, felt a burning sensation on the irons of his clogs. A big metal electric socket blew out, hitting her mother on the back of her neck. The fire range blew out and they all ran outside in terror. The family had to stay with neighbours for a week until repairs to Eastfield Farm had been completed.

No photographic souvenirs of childhood were ever made. There was no spare cash for such luxuries. But when you've loved someone as much as Mary loved Frisk, memories live on forever, never fading, as do photographs.

CHAPTER
FIVE

Irene

Irene Martin was born in 1920 at 3 Hill Terrace, Paddock. The eldest of nine children, Irene began her education at the church school when she was only three years old, walking there and back for dinner, which there wasn't much of. But her mother always baked a stone of flour every week, so at least they had good white bread. They drank a lot of cocoa.

Paddock Council School followed, from nine till twelve, and two till four-thirty. There was no attempt to camouflage poverty. "Irene Martin, come out and get your dinner ticket," Miss Linnaker called her name out along with others who walked to Eaton's Dining Rooms. Originally for working men, it also catered for schoolchildren from all over Huddersfield. They ate in a back room, standing up round a big wooden table. Irene always asked for rice and fruit after the main meal. There was water to drink.

At her home there were two bedrooms, with two double beds in one. Her parents slept in one, and the other had children top to toe, all scrabbling about to get a bit of the bedclothes. In cold weather overcoats were thrown over as well, and warm oven plates taken up to take off the icy chill. The lavatory was outside, but there was a bucket on the landing. As if there weren't enough bodies in the beds, there were often "bugs as big as ladybirds" too, so every now and then the bedsteads had creosote applied to kill them off.

Despite having no fridges, nobody seemed to get food poisoning. Irene thinks it was because they couldn't afford to lay out a lot of money on shopping in bulk. Therefore, when food was bought daily, it was fresh.

It was rather a dangerous practice, but before electric lighting was installed in the house, when Irene was left in charge of the other children she used to roll up a long piece of newspaper, light one end from the fire, then dash into the cellar for a shovel full of coal and hope she landed upstairs before it went out.

A few days before Christmas she was one of the children invited either to the Cinderella or Royds Hall School party for poor children. Irene always hoped she was allocated to Royds, because every girl received a doll there. Irene never thought about hanging a stocking up for Santa Claus. Father Christmas was somebody you saw "when you went to those dos" and that was it.

But she thought Whitsuntide was marvellous. Her mother bought "checks" weekly, then they were used to buy a print frock and a pair of white pumps from Wilton's at the top of Chapel Hill. Preening herself in these new acquisitions and showing off to neighbours and relations was rewarded by a penny being put into the little girl's new pocket. *Then* her mother usually finished up with it.

Unlike many children of that time, Irene didn't go to Sunday school. She just played out if it was fine, or sat at the bottom of the stairs with Louisa Fox, her best friend, when they lived next door to each other at Paddock. There they spent many happy hours playing with "scraps" — pretty pictures of animals and flowers, putting a pin between the folds of paper and hoping to win another scrap. Sometimes they walked to the Premier cinema or the Plaza. A child could go in for 1d and be given a bag of sweets as well.

Until she was ten, Irene had never been on holiday and never seen the sea. But in 1930 her Auntie May, who lived at Longwood, offered to take her as a companion for her daughter Connie. Blackpool, of course, was the destination. Furthermore, Auntie May had crocheted a beret for each child "out of that rabbit wool". The night before, Irene stayed at Auntie May's and never slept for excitement. They went by train, and stayed at Osborne Road, right next to the pleasure beach.

After tea in the boarding house, she and Connie, in their brand-new berets, sauntered round looking at the sideshows and rides. On the "front" a fellow played a piano, and crowds of holidaymakers stood round him singing hit songs of the day: Al Jolson's *Sonny Boy* and some of Gracie Fields' songs, such as *Sally* and *Sing As We Go*, to encourage people to buy the Lawrence Wright sheet music.

Dance tunes which had crowds happily waltzing round in the Tower Ballroom were lustily sung in the open air. *I'm Forever Blowing Bubbles, I'll Be Your Sweetheart* and *Three O'Clock In the Morning, We've Danced the Whole Night Through* were all popular.

In that heady atmosphere what did it matter if, in the real, everyday world, her dad was out of work, and liked to drink, and poor scholars sat at the front in school, with the cleverest at the back. What did it matter if Miss Linnaker scoffed, "Irene, you're not like your cousin"? Their lovely, fluffy berets were exactly alike, and if the fluff occasionally looked a bit flat, all they needed to do was blow on it and up it fluffed — just like the dandelion clocks growing in the meadows at home.

CHAPTER
SIX

The Odersfelt

How many remember the children's magazine *The Odersfelt*, for Huddersfield schoolchildren? At the opening of copies bound into a book is a photograph of the mayor, Ald. Law Taylor, JP, my great uncle. The mayor's letter, from the Mayor's Parlour, Town Hall, Huddersfield, January 1925, read:

My dear Friends,

On the occasion of the publication of the first issue of your School Magazine, the Editor has very kindly asked me if I would send a few words of greeting. I am delighted to comply with the request for several reasons. In the first place it enables me to say how pleased I was to receive the many reports of the delegates you appointed to attend the ceremony when I was elected Mayor on the 10th of November. They form very interesting reading, and I shall prize them very much indeed. I would like personally to thank all my little friends for attending. I am sure, from the reports, that they were all very much interested in the proceedings. I sincerely trust this interest may be maintained, and that every boy and girl who was present realized that the future governors of our towns and cities are now in the schools, and that they may have an incentive to take a closer part in the ceremony at some future date.

As the Mayor of the town I come into contact with all kinds of people and associations, but I can assure you that there is no section of the community that I am more interested in than the children. I want you all to appreciate fully all the possibilities that are in store for you. I want you all to grow up noble men and noble women. I want you all to love your parents, to love your brothers and sisters, and to love your school-mates and teachers.

I want you to be kind to the poor and to the sick, and to be gentle to the aged. I want you to be kind to all dumb animals and be a friend to them. To love the birds, and flowers, and nature. Try to realize that you are part of one great family, and that all boys and girls of whatever race or nationality are brothers and sisters, and should live peacefully together.

"Do noble deeds, not dream them all day long."

In addition, I want you to take full advantage of all the educational facilities which are now placed at your disposal. Seize every opportunity to improve your minds. Let it be your endeavour to obtain the fullest marks possible, and always think that your place should be at the top of your class. Bear in mind there is always room at the top.

There are many more things I would like to say but space forbids. I send you all my kindest greetings. To all the teachers I would send a word of cheer and encouragement in the noble work in which they are engaged. They have the destinies of the future generations in their hands. I am sure the trust will not be mis-placed. I wish your Magazine all success. I trust it may have a beneficial effect upon the lives and characters of the children of our schools. Again thanking you, and extending all good wishes.

Believe me,
  Yours sincerely,
    LAW TAYLOR

Schoolchildren found it a challenge to come up with stories, wit and humour, hopefully to be printed in their magazine. The jokes reflect the era. Evelyn Jagger sent this one:

MOTHER: "Why are you letting Baby eat blotting paper?"
TOMMY: "Well, Mother, he's just swallowed some ink, so I thought it would blot it up."

Dorothy Lee was successful with this effort:

RONALD: "Why did the ham roll, Uncle?"
UNCLE JACK: "I'm sure I don't know, my boy. Why?"
RONALD: "Because it saw the apple turnover!"

Nine-year-old Stanley Poyner had the right idea with this poem:

BE A SPORT

If you ever have a hump,
　　Do not pull a face;
Try to hop and skip and jump,
　　Or have a glorious race.
If you ever have bad luck
　　And sit down on a thistle,
Sing a song and show some pluck;
　　If you can't — well, whistle.
If you want to be a sport
　　You will have to try, and try;
I would not be the other sort —
　　It's horrid form to cry.

The magazine provided schools' cricket notes, and girls' games, namely stoolball. There was information about the Yorkshire Schools' rugby final, and a piece about the boys of the Hillhouse Council School winning the "Hoyle" cup after a very keenly contested game with the other finalists, St Patrick's RC School. Cricketing idols gave advice about the game — and life — to the school magazine. A letter dated 23 April 1925 reads:

TO THE SCHOOLBOYS OF HUDDERSFIELD

Dear Young Friends,

It has often struck me, when I have seen boys playing in cricket fields, what better facilities they now have than boys had in my younger days, when they had to steal into any rough corner of a field, only to be chased out again by the farmer. I should like to remind you that Cricket Clubs who grant you the privilege of playing in their fields expect you to repay them by diligent practice, and by qualifying to be the future members of their teams.

Another thing that has appealed to me is the great interest taken in the boys' games by their teachers.

My duties now are with boys and young men. The coach, like the teacher, can only point out the way things should be done — it is left to the pupil to do his best to carry out the advice that is given. Unless the pupil is keen, no progress will be made; the same applies in the field as in the school.

Remember above all, to "Play Cricket".

Keep the game as clean as possible.

Take all decisions that are given, whether you think they are right or not.

Never leave the field feeling that you have taken a mean advantage of your opponents, or that your opponents have done the same.

Play for your side first and last.

If you fail to get runs with the bat you can assist your bowlers by being alert.

Team work will win without brilliant stars.

If you cannot be a winner, be a good loser, and leave smiling.

Trusting that you will satisfy yourselves and your associates, and have a happy season.

I am, Yours Very Sincerely,
GEORGE HERBERT HIRST

Pep talks such as those by G.H. Hirst would not go awry in any era.

But children do like plenty of jokes among the seriousness of life. More from the 1925 *Odersfelt*:

MOTHER: "Johnny, if you eat any more you'll burst."
JOHNNY: "Never mind, Mother dear, just hand me the cake and stand clear."

How about this for a lottery?

TEACHER: "Now, Sam, do you know what a saddle is?"
SAM: "No, sir."
TEACHER: "Then what is it your father puts on a horse each day?"
SAM: "A bob each way, sir."

Finally, a sign of the times.

PASSENGER: "Do you think the motor-car means the extinction of the horse?"
MOTORIST: "Oh, no — not if the horse gets out of the way in time."

CHAPTER
SEVEN

Sydney

Some tend to think of "Get on your bike" as modern advice when looking for a job. But Sydney Pike's father, Harry, did just that back in the 1920s, cycling daily from Burnley to Huddersfield, whatever the weather. His family stayed behind with an aunt until Harry was established in work as a brass moulder at Hopkinson's.

Originally from Workington, the family lived with Auntie Cissie until Dad found rooms for them at Nunn's Commercial House in Huddersfield. They lived below ground level in a cellar dwelling, yet the bedroom was on the top floor, three floors up. They didn't have gas, only paraffin lamps, so Harry devised a kind of cylinder about 18 inches long by 6 inches in diameter, and fashioned a holder to fix to the wall so they could have gaslight. After being out one evening there was a smell of acetylene in the room. "For God's sake don't strike a match!" yelled Harry. The owner of the rooming house had been tampering with the contraption in their absence.

Life took a turn for the better when Mrs Pike, reading the local *Examiner* newspaper, saw an advert for a cottage to rent near Bradley Gate Farm. It was an odd kind of place, with two cellars, one below the other, but it would be a home. Back went Harry to Burnley, to bring household goods, including a flock mattress which he strapped onto his bike.

The cottage, in a rural setting up the winding "Old Lane", had a small Yorkshire range in the living room, a recess for a water tap, a stone sink in the cellar, and an outside lavatory. There were twigs galore in Newhouse Wood to light the fire, and freedom to play there in complete safety.

Sydney, the "baby" of the family, didn't dare venture into the lower cellar. There was an ominous loose flag down there, which squelched if stood on. His dad, Harry, was in his element making the cottage into as comfortable a little home as possible with limited means. He built a cupboard from old packing cases and wood scrap.

In the tiny scullery was an oval-shaped table set on a pedestal, and they had an ornament of a boy and girl under a glass dome, seated on a pastel-coloured rock, the boy looking up at the girl, who sat forever with a crochet hook in her hand, waiting to begin her work.

There was a scrap of carpet on the stone floor in the living room. Mrs Pike freshened it up by scattering wet tea leaves on it, then going down on her hands and knees with a brush and shovel to sweep them up with the dust. They hadn't a vacuum cleaner. In any case, one would only have taken up valuable space. Mrs Pike believed in "looking on the bright side". With the oil lamp lit in winter time, and a blazing coal and wood fire, what more could anyone desire?

When he first came to Huddersfield in search of work, Harry went begging at farms. But when the family rented the little cottage alongside Newhouse Wood they thought it Heaven on earth. Mrs Pike adored cleaning the glass bowl containing an oil lamp, her wedding ring clicking against the glass.

Working in the brass foundry at Hopkinson's, Harry was strategically placed to create a number of household items, such as fretted brass flat-iron stands, a couple of brass shoehorns, and a bicycle chain. On the mantelpiece in the cottage were proudly displayed two solid brass candlesticks — an heirloom from Sydney's Grandad.

Saturdays were magical from beginning to end for young Sydney: playing in the wood during the daytime, then shopping with his parents in town after tea. Sydney and his dad zigzagged round the toy shops while his mother hung around the butchers and greengrocers on Shambles Lane until food was sold off cheaply just before closing time.

Sydney thought he had a far better time with his dad, looking round the magnificent toy display in Rushworth's. Sometimes something was bought for him — perhaps a toy cap gun or a packet of pretend cigarettes. A conductor on a tram, seeing the boy with one of these sweets in his mouth, called out, "D' you wanna light, lad?"

Saturday evening entertainment was varied. It may be the second house of the Palace, or the cinema. Once, up in the "gods" at the Tudor, there was pandemonium when the audience leapt to their feet on hearing what they thought to be a fire alarm. Among Mrs Pike's wicker basket of shopping, on the floor beneath her seat, was an alarm clock she had bought, never thinking to enquire whether or not it was wound up. It was the type with two big bells on top, clanging away enough to waken the dead. Mr Pike was more wound up than the clock after that embarrassing experience.

There were no street lights up the old lane, so on dark winter nights if they were going out, Harry, who could turn his hand to anything, put a candle in a coach lamp and placed it behind the wall. Nights out ended with a bag of chips each from Oddy's on Sheepridge. They were scrumptious with plenty of salt, pepper and vinegar, wrapped up tightly — apart from the opening at the top — in an old copy of the *Examiner*.

Every night they heard footsteps walking round the cottage. Returning from "the flicks" one Saturday night, they bumped into the local policeman. "Oh, it's you that's putting t'wind up us, is it?" laughed Harry. The bobby-on-the-beat was checking that all was in order.

There was a bit of lawn, and in the summer an old tartan travelling rug was put out for the boys to play on. A pal, Peter Tillotson, who lived nearby in a bungalow down Wiggan Lane, used to bring his clockwork Hornby train. Happy hours went by playing with trains and signal-boxes after school. Buttercups, daisies and bluebells made the surrounding woods a pastoral delight. Little caterpillars hanging from trees in the wood were a menace though, catching on hair and giving the girls a fright.

A mystical, magic aura was almost palpable in the days up to Christmas, when the Pike family sought bargains in town. Sydney adored watching the Hornby trains going round a track in Rushworth's toy department, knowing he wouldn't be having one, but nevertheless he was without envy and simply joyful at being able to watch. Just to look was enough. One year, however, Santa did leave him a Double Nought Meccano set. In 1929 they cost 10s.

There were no such frivolities as fancy wrapping paper. Sydney thought Father Christmas had really let him down one year when, at the side of his bed, reposed a cardboard carton with the words PALETHORPE'S SAUSAGES printed across it. But on opening it he was delighted with loads of cheap tin toys, and a long thin selection box. Sydney's brother, Gordon, had a "Daisy" air rifle from Barker's in Huddersfield. It shot real lead pellets. He used it most mornings, his target being a mouse which fled beneath the sideboard.

Every Christmas Eve the boys went carol singing at Newhouse Hall, walking through Newhouse Wood in total darkness unless there was a moon. A local JP, Mr T.P. Crosland, lived there and his housekeeper, Miss Davis, had instructions to take a goose — carrying it by its neck — early on Christmas Eve to Mr and Mrs Pike.

The vegetable garden belonging to the Hall adjoined Harry's garden. Growing vegetables was a great help in eking out a living. They were healthy, too. On Saturday mornings Harry walked over to the Hall to pay the 7s 6d a week rent for the cottage.

The family always had a party at Christmas with lots of games. Spin the Bottle was a favourite. When an empty pop bottle stopped spinning, whoever it pointed to had to kiss the bottle-spinner. Old-timers like Murder and Postman's Knock vied with Winkums in popularity when the three boys were older.

For Winkums each boy stood behind a seated girl. They had to wink at a girl without being noticed. If the wink was seen, a forfeit was demanded. When all the forfeits were collected, one player shut his or her eyes, so they would not know who owned the article. "Here's a thing and a very fine thing, who is the owner of this fine thing, and what has he to do?" they said, dangling the handkerchief, tie, or whatever forfeit had been surrendered. "Go outside and shout 'Fried herrings' ten times" was about as daring as those merrymakers of the 1930s got. It mattered not, as only the trees and wildlife in Newhouse Wood were there to listen.

Enticing aromas filled the little home on Sunday mornings. Mrs Pike had a huge frying pan which she covered with eggs and bacon. A black kettle was always on the hob. Attached to the fender were a couple of buffets which housed shoe-cleaning tackle.

Tibbs, the tabby cat, had to fend for itself apart from scraps thrown from plates, and milk. It used to sit on one of the fireside buffets and make sudden darts after a mouse which dared to poke its nose through a crack. Living alongside woods and fields there were many mice, as well as rabbits. More than once a dead animal gave a fright to the person entering the outside privy.

There was always room for anyone who called, and even Auntie Cissie stayed one Christmas. "We worked it out someway," said Sydney. All were willing to "give and take". They ate simple food, such as mushy peas and pork pies, and a quarter of polony with dollops of mustard livening up thick "doorsteps" of bread. Collops were another favourite on winter teatimes.

Winter passed, as did dire poverty. Sydney's parents managed to buy a pair of black pumps for him from the Co-op drapery department. They cost about half a crown, and he swore he could run twice as fast in them.

The family sent for a pink-backed catalogue, with instructions that it be "left in the coal hole" if nobody was at home when it arrived. A navy blue serge suit was ordered from it for Sydney. He enjoyed copying pictures in the catalogue, drawing them on any old bit of paper or backs of envelopes. Tracing was another enjoyable pastime. One 1930s summer, brother Gordon, who had a bicycle bought from the catalogue, cycled to see his grandparents in Cumberland, wearing his Boy Scout uniform and buying food at farms. There wasn't a hitch until he was almost home. He called at Oddy's for fish and chips and got a puncture.

Mrs Pike was excellent at "making ends meet". Cumbrian "Taty Hot Pot", layers of thinly cut potatoes with slices of onion, baked in the oven until the top layer was golden brown, was a meal fit for a king, especially with a few drops of Yorkshire Relish sauce. Also tripe and onions cooked in milk, and rabbit pies, with a couple of egg cups under the top pastry to keep it from sagging.

All manner of marvellous items could be acquired by diligently saving up coupons from commodities such as tea. Mrs Pike had her first electric iron after saving the required amount of Redman's tea coupons.

Mr Pike was "always at back o' t'queue" when new clothes were mooted, but considered himself lucky to have a home, and was thankful just for his children to be decently clothed. He had a melodeon which he loved to play, his work, the woods, a happy family life, and tunes of the twenties and thirties to whistle — what more could a man want? And to go for moonlight walks through Newhouse Wood was an unimaginable delight, which didn't cost a penny either.

At Easter time Mrs Pike decorated eggs fresh from the nearby farm by wrapping them in onion skins and boiling them. They ended up with unique mottled patterns, then William, the artist of the family, painted faces on them with Indian ink.

Finances picked up enough for the family to visit the seaside in the summer school holidays for one glorious week. But few holidays escape without a trauma of some sort. Mrs Pike made sandwiches for the train journey and put them in a brown carrier bag with bottles of pop. Sydney was detailed to carry that. Alas, poor Sydney. Another identical carrier bag was on the table, with eggs at the top; provisions for Gordon, who had elected to stay at home. Sydney thought they were hard-boiled eggs for the journey, and picked up the wrong bag. They had to go under the railway subway and queue for the train. Little Sydney kept putting the bag down, then inched forward another step or two, by which time the eggs had cracked, and there was a trail of broken eggs behind the astonished lad. His mother played hell with him.

Bridlington was all the sweeter when eventually they arrived, having not eaten or had a drink since leaving home. After settling into the boarding house with a welcoming cup of tea and biscuits, they went out to book for shows. Spirits miraculously soared, so much so that they could even laugh about the incident. For there was the Spa Theatre, Floral Hall, Sewerby Park, fishing, sails round the bay, going to look at the lifeboats. The week had just begun. Paradise!

At the end of Marshall Avenue, where the family stayed, was a chap with a wind-up gramophone playing *When I Grow Too Old To Dream* over and over again. A little terrier dog sat on a pram by the side of the gramophone howling an accompaniment. The gramophone had one of those big horns, and Sydney wondered if the dog was the original of the one pictured looking down the horn on His Master's Voice records.

Despondency as the holiday drew to a close was tempered by the hope that they may be able to have a day excursion to Blackpool later in the year. Altham's shop in Huddersfield had leaflets on a string, advertising trips.

On reflection, there was a lot to be said for going home. Sydney's pal, Peter Tillotson, would be waiting anxiously for his return, to hear all about the Great Adventure and resume their games together. There was a stick of rock for him in the case. Sydney looked forward on the train home to their games of make believe. Up-ending chairs to face each other, in imagination they became a submarine, a rocket or racing cars. The brass kettle stand made an imposing steering wheel. The hissing and whistling of the steam train had Sydney thinking with pleasure of the reunion. The boys created their own sound effects, but "driving at speed round bends" taxed their throats. A gramophone record playing *Colonel Bogey* was exactly right for marching round when being "Soldiers of the King". With their dads' red spotted handkerchiefs swathed round their foreheads, and black patches over one eye, they were pirates. Bits of broken fencing made admirable swords. If they felt like being Indians, a couple of doormats tied with string round their legs and birds' feathers stuck on a band round their heads were ideal.

On Saturday mornings there were "errands to run", though they certainly weren't *run* on the homeward journey. Weighted down with a stone of flour, "taties" and other groceries, it was a hot, tiring trudge from the shops at Sheepridge back up the winding lane.

Mrs Pike sometimes worked at the Masonic Hall in South Parade, helping in the kitchen. One Burns Night the haggis had been piped in, then someone ordered, "Send a bottle down for the kitchen staff." She always tried to catch the last tram home, and Harry went to fetch his wife that night. She was so unaccountably "wuzzy" she couldn't find the tram step, so it was deemed more sensible to walk home, via Alder Street, trusting in the fresh air to sober her up.

By the time of the Second World War the family had moved to Wiggan Lane. They had an air-raid shelter, but it had water down at the bottom. Harry dug a sump in one corner and made a water pump with a rod attached. Bent to the shape of a handle, the hose pipe could be worked up and down. it was a crude affair, but it served the purpose. Always a "knackler", Harry could probably have been an inventor. He decided to fix up an electric heater in the Anderson shelter, running it from the house. But if the electric heater had fallen into the watery base of the shelter, the Pike family would have been despatched into the next world with no help from a German bomb or doodlebug.

Ideas and ingenuity made for a far more fulfilling life than having pots of money and simply being able to buy what was wanted. Those with money to throw away missed out on so many good things in life. Walking home from the pictures, pausing for "a fish and a penn'orth" which tasted much better in the cold night air than waiting to eat them inside. Laughing and talking with others on the way home — something you can't do when in a car. Chance encounters, the unpredictability of life. Innocently causing all hell to break loose in the Tudor cinema when the newly bought alarm clock did as it was meant to do — and clanged like billy-o dead on seven o'clock. That would never have happened had the family been affluent enough to take the shopping home first by car. So really, there was much more fun in being short of "a bit of the ready".

CHAPTER
EIGHT

Denis

One of Denis Boothroyd's boyhood pranks was to tie a box up with cotton, keeping the end of the cotton in his hand while he hid behind a wall, then lie in gleeful anticipation for a curious, acquisitive passer-by. First there was the look of surprise that a parcel or box had been abandoned on the pavement, then a furtive glance round to see if he or she was being observed, then the decision to bend down and either open it or hurry off home with the tantalizing parcel. At the exact moment an eager hand was outstretched to get hold of the article, it began to move of its own accord. Such a different expression on the victim's features! One of "I wouldn't take anything that didn't belong to me" combined with a speedy retreat. The game never failed to have Denis howling with laughter in true Bunter of Greyfriars style as he nipped over the wall and re-positioned the empty parcel.

Born in 1922 in Lepton, Denis was also an addict of "Tin Can Squat", which he played with the other village lads. A large empty Bartlett pears tin or big treacle tin was ideal, and the roads were free of traffic apart from the occasional horse and cart in the 1920s.

To see a motor car was an event. The tin was placed in the road, with the boy in charge of it counting to a hundred while the others scattered in different directions to hide. Tin Can Squat shouted "Ready" after counting a hundred as fast as he could, then raced off in search of his pals. When one was found, both ran like mad to get to the tin first. The winner kicked the tin, roared "Tin Can Squat", and so the game went on.

Football was played in the streets as well as in fields, there being no danger from traffic. There was no spare money to buy special shorts when Denis joined a local team, so his mother made some from old bits of navy material.

Mr Boothroyd cobbled the family's shoes. Denis liked wearing clogs, and rubbed candle fat on the irons to make them — and him — whizz along faster when the roads were icy in winter. It was also a marvellous sensation to make sparks fly off his clogs. Proper football boots couldn't be budgeted for either, but his dad nailed strips of leather beneath his son's ordinary boots instead of the studded football boots.

The Boothroyds preferred Llandudno for their annual summer seaside holiday, but Denis had to wait until the Monday to take his bucket and spade onto the sands. Sunday was for worship, and no games of any description could be played. So Denis wore his Sunday-best suit to attend the outdoor service at St Tudno's Church, and thoroughly enjoyed the novelty of singing rousing hymns in the open air. Besides, it was good to feel smart. Doris, his sister, loved wearing a pretty dress and straw bonnet, and her string of beads.

They "kept themselves" at the boarding house, buying food in local shops and taking it in for the landlady to cook. Sunday dinnertime was invariably a joint of meat, potatoes and vegetables, followed by rice pudding. Some evenings after tea Denis enjoyed skimming pebbles across the sea. But even that innocent pastime was outlawed on Sundays.

The rules of the house were displayed on a list in the bedrooms. Breakfast between 8 and 8.30 a.m., dinner at 1 p.m. — unless families were having a packed lunch on the beach — and tea at 5 p.m. Each family was assigned a shelf in the huge sideboard in the dining room for their breakfast marmalade and sundry items. There was an extra charge of 6d for use of the cruet. Guests weren't encouraged to stay in the house after breakfast or any other time of the day until evening, as there was all the cleaning and tidying up to attend to, so over breakfast all eyes were turned anxiously to the skies, wondering if the sun would shine. If it didn't, mackintoshes and sou'westers were put on, and holidaymakers set off for a brisk walk in the teeth of a gale or mothers took their knitting onto the "front" to pass the time chatting in a shelter sitting on those hard, slatted forms until the drizzle passed over. The children had a comic or cheap little book to amuse themselves with, or on weekdays there was always that old standby, looking round the shops, and buying presents for neighbours, friends and relatives at home. It was better to buy something that lasted, rather than rock, because they remembered you'd bought them something then.

On Sunday afternoon there was the unmissable sedate walk round the Great Orme. Everyone was in their Sunday finery, the ladies eyeing each other's dresses and hats. Sometimes conversation with complete strangers would be engaged in, and perhaps an arrangement made for children to meet next morning and play together on the sands.

Once or twice the Boothroyds tried Scarborough for a change — there were "some grand big 3*d* ice-cream cornets from the Corner Café on the front" — and they visited Blackpool illuminations in the autumn, but Llandudno remained their firm favourite. Yet Denis wasn't really bothered where he was, as long as he could have a fried egg sandwich for supper.

CHAPTER
NINE

Jennie

Also born in Lepton in 1923 was Jennie Mallinson, at Greave House Terrace. When her Grandma was widowed, it was only natural that she moved in with the family. Jennie was an only child, so when her parents were busy working in their fish and chip shop Grandma stayed in and taught her all sorts of things, about life, and knitting, and going outside and bowing nine times to the new moon to ensure good fortune.

The house was only four doors away from the mortuary, which was under the council offices, and Jennie wasn't keen on that at all. Lying in bed unable to sleep, knowing what was lying within a stone's throw, may have caused her to sleep walk. But more often than not she crept out of bed and climbed in with her Grandma. They had a lot in common, including a liking for "nice mucky fat" from the joint, pickled beetroot (they boiled it themselves, much nicer than ready bought) and bread for cosy suppers together.

It was a supremely contented, happy childhood. Everybody in the village cared for each other, and they could pop next door and leave their own door wide open. They could have a "cal" — Yorkshire for gossip or telling a tale — and everything would still be "in apple pie order" on their return. The greengrocer who came round selling his wares stored his vegetables in a hut where they were as safe as houses. He had boxes of oranges tied round with a thick, strong, plaited kind of straw, which was ideal for skipping ropes.

Oh, that French skipping! — "running in" when the girl at each side of the rope twined it the same way meant that the skipper needed plenty of dexterity. But when *two* ropes were used, they had to watch both the rope approaching and the other going away. Any child capable of achieving that deserved either a medal or at least a bag of Yorkshire Mixtures, those prettily coloured hard-boiled sweets, some in the shape of fish with gaping, pink mouths.

In 1931 Jennie was thrilled to be a bridesmaid for her auntie, who was supposed to be rather good at sewing. She made Jennie's dress in artificial silk, with a matching fashionable Dutch bonnet. The rim and side bits were held out with wire. The dress felt slightly restricted at the back, and rather tight even for Jennie's slight figure. In the taxi on the way to the church she leant forward to look out of the window, and the row of press studs all the way down the back popped open, one by one. It didn't show on the photographs though.

Mr Mallinson saved half a crown a week towards summer holiday week, reckoning that £7 would cover the lot, at 3s 6d a night for "a family room". The rest took care of the fare, food and spending money.

A bright, intelligent child, Jennie passed the 11-plus examination and went to Greenhead High School for girls in 1934. Though the emphasis was on academic subjects, they did have domestic science too. First formers were instructed to take a gentleman's handkerchief for the first lesson, to formally learn how to wash and iron correctly. Notes had to be made on the procedure. The next week was more intricate — a serviette, or napkin as the linen ones were known, had to be dealt with in similar fashion. Laundering was a science. Until then, girls had only known their mothers dealing with peggy tubs and the big rollers on mangles.

A whole new world was opening up to them at the High School. Before long, making a dressing gown was on the agenda. Jennie's mother bought a type of red ripple cloth from the Yorkshire Warehouse, at 2s 11d a yard.

Some pupils stayed at Greenhead for school dinner, and a few took their own food to be warmed up then eaten in the science room. One girl took a 2d tin of Heinz baked beans to be heated for her midday meal every day of the school week.

Jennie preferred to go home, even though it was a rush. The school gong boomed at ten past twelve. Indoor shoes had to be changed for sturdy lace-up outdoor ones, and coat, hat and gloves were put on in the cloakroom. Then there was the run down to Lord Street to catch the quarter to one petrol bus to Lepton. Home for one, then the half past one bus back to town.

It made a change from the formality of the school regime. Or could it have been the crushes that Jennie kept having on bus conductors? After all, if a Greenhead High School girl so much as *looked* at a college boy she'd be put in detention, and the possibility of being hauled before headmistress Miss Hill was even worse. At least chatting with a bus conductor there was *some* male contact. The only male in the vicinity of school was Mr Atkinson, the caretaker.

All the girls, especially if they were in the Junior or Senior choirs, regarded Speech Day as the highlight of the school year. Rules were strict, as with ordinary uniform. All had to wear white dresses for Speech Day, *not* cream ones. No jewellery, rings or earrings were allowed. En masse in the Town Hall they certainly looked all the more impressive unadorned. Why gild the lily?

Good manners, courtesy and "Honour Before Honours", the school motto, were instilled into pupils from the very first day. When a mistress or any other adult entered a room, girls had to respectfully stand, and not sit down until told to do so. There was a long tradition of *crème de la crème* about the girls who attended Greenhead High School, especially in academic and music pursuits.

Jennie was a typical, shining example of the type of pupil Miss Hill cherished. Always at the top of her form, except once, when, only attaining second place, Jennie's mother asked, "What have you been doing, only second, Jennie?" In School Certificate examinations Jennie obtained eight credits and a distinction. Miss Hill wanted her to continue at college then university, but finances wouldn't allow it.

However, life may not have turned out as well had she flown the nest and spread her wings. For at school,

61

when queuing outside secretary Miss Haigh's door for the two tickets allowed parents for Speech Day, Jennie Mallinson was always towards the end of the queue because of the initial letter of her surname. She vowed that if ever she married, it would be to someone with a surname at the beginning. Her dream came true, for she married Denis Boothroyd, the boy who used to love to play "Tin Can Squat", and their favourite English seaside resort is still Llandudno.

CHAPTER
TEN

A 1934 Miscellany

What goes on in the wider world beyond an individual childhood has an impact. It provides a background against which lives are lived. For instance, in January 1934 came a warning that women who swilled their flags and half their street because a neighbour poured a bucket full over hers, may find themselves lacking water for necessities. At Great Universal Stores a winter sale offered over 3,000 frocks and coats at "an amazingly low price of 7s 6d each". The mayor's Boots for Bairns Fund Ball, tickets 10s 6d each, had music for dancing provided by Billy Hobson and his Orchestra. The town hall was transformed into a fairyland of beautiful flowers and myriad lights, with a room set aside for those who preferred to play bridge.

"Scullery houses" at Carr Street, Marsh, with three bedrooms and a tiled bathroom, were £425, including lease and streetage charges. Winter meant taking extra precautions with health, and Virol cod liver oil and malt was the daily dose for many children. Nasty tastes could always be forgotten by a visit to the pictures. The previous year, Joan Blondell and Ruby Keeler made *Gold Diggers of 1933* supported by Ginger Rogers,

Dick Powell and Guy Kibbee. At the Grand, Tom Walls and Ralph Lynn starred in *Cuckoo In the Nest* and at the Empire, Stanley Lupino and Thelma Todd were in *You Made Me Love You.*

Children aged from seven to twelve, whose fathers were employed at British Dyestuffs Corporation, went to a matinée performance at the Palace Theatre that January. There were 450 of them, and after the show they went to the Victoria Hall Café for tea. At the end of the treat each child was given a box of chocolates.

Every child enjoys being frightened, as long as there's a guarantee it's only make believe. *King Kong*, starring Fay Wray and Robert Armstrong, was on at the Waterloo. Children could not be admitted unless accompanied by an adult. I remember going to see it, and pictured myself being carried through a jungle for days afterwards, cradled in the hairy arms of King Kong. Maybe if Fay Wray had been fatter King Kong would not have been able to gather her to his bosom so easily. The Potato Marketing Board announced that the latest women's craze was for "curves", and if they could get more women turning in that direction they would get more potatoes sold.

Ralph Cuthbert's chemist's shop was burgled and articles to the value of £80 taken. The stolen goods included two perfume sprays, a valet outfit, powder compacts, seven fountain pens, a pair of theatre glasses, two pocket barometers and a flash lamp.

Mackintoshes could be bought for 4s 9d at the Yorkshire Warehouse on Cross Church Street. Wool frocks were 9s 11d. Rushworth's on Westgate corner were selling jumper suits at 29s 11d and 25s 11d, washable doeskin gloves at 2s 11d, and down quilts were half price at 19s 11d to 68s 3d. In the sale were hookside corsets at 15s.

In the market, plaice was 1s 4d per lb, lemon sole was 1s 2d to 1s 10d per lb. English turkeys were 1s 2d per lb, geese 1s 3d per lb, and pheasants 8s 6d to 9s a brace. Cauliflowers were 10d to 1s each, and kidney beans 1s 6d per lb.

Only a penny tram ride from town, on Broad Lane Estate, Dalton, were houses for sale at £365 and £375. There were also some detached houses with three bedrooms for £425. Repayments were 9s per week.

Courtesy of the Cinderella Society, Mr Edward Haigh took 200 children to Blackpool in six Hanson buses. They were supplied with ham sandwiches, as most would not have had any breakfast. The party arrived at 11.30 a.m. and enjoyed one and a half hours on the sands with a few donkey rides, followed by a good dinner in the Tower Café and excellent seats at the circus. Finally, tea was provided and the party arrived back home in Huddersfield at nine, after the happiest day of their lives. It was Thursday, 5 April 1934. That weekend Bradley Villa Farm was used as an aerodrome, and the North British Aviation Company gave flying displays.

It was learned that the hottest temperatures during the previous years had been on 3 June and 5 July, when it reached 87°. By April 1934 a public notice proclaimed "Save Water: Reservoirs only 1/3 full". But eggs were still a shilling a dozen, and the most popular car colour that season was black.

One of the most popular stores in the 1930s was "Woollies" — Woolworths, the "Nothing Over Sixpence" store. When my mother went into town I looked forward to her bringing back a sixpenny Shirley Temple dressing doll book, or chunky sixpenny *Life and Times of Shirley Temple*. Later on I was fascinated with the counter piled high with film star magazines, such as *Picture Goer* and *Picture Show*, full of articles and photographs of idols of the silver screen. Some used to take the magazines to the hairdresser, and ask for a certain style. Recently I spoke with a lady who used to work at Woolworths when it was the beloved "Nothing Over Sixpence" store. Betty first worked in a mill, but hated it. Only fourteen when she left school, she learned that Woolworths were wanting assistants to work on Friday evenings and all day Saturday till nine at night. The wage was 12s 6d. How delighted she was when the manager selected her to work full time, on the ice-cream counter!

At first, her mother went with her as an escort, collecting her at the close of the day's work too, "'Cos you never knew what can happen on Shambles Lane". Working on the ice-cream counter, Betty wore a white overall and white headband with a red initial "W" on the front. Assistants on other counters wore maroon with fawn collars. Cost of the overalls was deducted from the weekly wage until they were paid for. Wafers cost 3d or 4d, and there was always one on view on a slab. Cornets cost 1d or 2d. When the refrigerators closed down from September to Easter, Betty served on various other counters, such as horticulture, ribbons and laces, and sixpenny Dinkie cars. Now those "tanner" toys are collectors' items. Pure silk stockings were 6d each leg. Customers used to sometimes buy three at a time, in case one laddered. Café au lait was a popular shade, and ladies bought a lot of Pinnacle brand flesh-coloured stockings.

Spectacle wearers could pop into "Woollies" for new glasses. Even at only 6d a pair, there was frequently a great deal of indecision, as much as goes into the purchase of a pair nearer £100 sixty years on. Assistants had to ask customers to read columns of letters, decreasing in size, and give their "expert" advice when asked "Are they gold?" and "Do they suit me?"

Woolworths employees were entitled to a fortnight annual holiday, and one of the weeks was with pay. When a girl had worked there six months, she was also entitled to a 10s 6d "Christmas Box", rising to a magnificent £5 as years of service increased.

What a wonderful atmosphere those early Woolworth stores had — there was no need to hesitate whether one could afford to go in. If you had "a tanner" then something could be bought. It was such a draw with Saturday afternoon shoppers that crowds surged round the counters in droves. A girl need look no further for boyfriends if she worked there, as lots of young men sauntered in and out, as much to survey the pretty young assistants as what they were selling.

Officially, "Woollies" closed at nine on Christmas Eve, but shoppers dashed in and out in a fever of festive excitement for last-minute gifts and decorations sometimes up to midnight, according to Betty. Volunteers among the staff to stock-take on New Year's Day were paid double time.

In the 1930s snow didn't halt assistants getting to work on time. Trams never stopped for snow, recalled the ex-Woolworth sales assistant.

But alas, should a girl announce that she intended to marry, she had to leave the "Nothing Over Sixpence" store, as no married women were employed. "Miss Waddington" was heartbroken when her turn came to say goodbye to the friendly hustle and bustle of work.

Happy Days.

CHAPTER
ELEVEN

Betty and Joan

"Ding Dong Bell, Pussy's in the Well" is a nursery rhyme calculated to strike terror into the heart, but what hysteria erupted when little Betty Fullaway of Trough Farm, Mount Tabor, near Halifax, did nearly drown in a well in the yard one day in the 1920s.

Water had to be drawn from the well for all the household chores. Betty and her cousin Gilbert were fooling around one afternoon when the urge to give his cousin a push overwhelmed Gilbert. Only Betty's hair could be seen as her body was submerged. Her mother was busy in the house, but a guardian angel, in the form of the coalman, puffed and panted onto the scene carrying a sack of coal.

"What's up, lad?" he asked Gilbert, who was crying and pointing to the well. Quicker than lightning the coalman grabbed Betty's hair then yanked her shoulders, dragging her out. Had he not appeared at that moment the child most certainly would have drowned.

Elsie, Betty's mother, had to lower a bucket on a rope into the well when water was needed. Apart from isolated incidents such as the well near-fatality, she considered those years of early married life at Trough Farm as the happiest of them all. There were beautiful views over the Dean Valley, and no neighbours to intrude on the splendid isolation and loveliness of the place. Charles, her husband, was an engineer at the GPO, and they had two pretty little daughters, Betty and Joan, followed by a son, John William.

Outside was a large wash-house. Water had to be "carted" into the boiler to heat when it was wash day, then back again, bucket after bucket full, into the wash-house.

But when work was over for the day, and Charles was at home in the evenings, how delightful it was to relax and listen to the records on the new cabinet gramophone he had bought. The children loved to dance to the tunes, such as *The Wedding of the Painted Doll* and *Daddy Wouldn't Buy Me a Bow-wow*. The lovely *Carolina Moon* and *Charmaine* were played over and over again. Betty and Joan recited poems they had learnt at school. Lighting was by oil lamps and everything looked so cosy, inviting and homely in the firelight on autumn and winter evenings.

At bedtime the children were taken upstairs by their mother, carrying one of the lamps. When she went back downstairs, and the rooms were shrouded in complete darkness, Betty told ghost stories to Joan, who at first revelled in snuggling beneath the blankets and eiderdown for a while. Then, as the ghost stories became progressively more lurid and terrifying, even with the blankets drawn tightly round and her eyes screwed up tight, nothing seemed to provide protection from those "invisible beings" who might pounce down on her at any moment. She cried out for her mother, which only brought her to the bottom of the stairs, with a sharp clapping of hands and a stern "Go to sleep."

Arguments erupted when Betty and Joan had a bath together. A block of green Fairy soap was the chosen dirt remover, and both little girls wanted to touch the imprint of the "fairy" in its nappy first, before it was washed off and worn away to a flat nothing. Moving the hand over the imprinted figure had a sensuous pleasure not to be denied on bath night.

If the children were naughty the punishment was for them to stand in a corner of the living room, face to the wall, until the penalty was deemed to have been paid, and a "sorry" been said. The gramophone music playing as their parents gazed into the fire one evening, when Betty was in disgrace for some misdemeanour or other, made them quite forget about the little figure in the corner, until Joan exclaimed, "Betty's asleep standing up!" All was forgiven at once, and she was given a big hug.

Their mother always maintained "spare the rod and spoil the child", not taking the meaning of "rod" literally, but allowing children to misbehave without discipline meant they grew up into being "not nice people to know".

Trough Farm was not a "working farm" but they did have a few hens and chickens. In winter the little chickens were taken indoors to keep them warm. Joan fell over one and it died. Winter may have been cosy, but it did seem to have more hazards than summertime.

Sunday school was at Little Mission three miles away. The children often called to see Grandma Fullerton, who lived in a cottage nearby. Grandma could neither read nor write, but had a big metal trunk upstairs which was full of postcards from friends and relations all over the world. Joan and Betty loved looking at those on Sundays. There were no toys to play with at Grandma's.

Joan was born on 25 June 1925. When aged three, she hated being left when Betty went to school, so one day when she was crying and wailing, "Want to go with Betty, want to go to school", her mother said, "Oh all right, take her with you then."

Two lots of sandwiches were made and two cans of milk, straight from the cow. Betty carried the refreshments in a round wicker basket, and Joan was allowed to stay, but for that day only.

Betty was the only child allowed to stay at school for her dinner, as it was too far for her to go home and be back in time for afternoon class. Miss Fielding refused to warm a drink for her, as other pupils might then have wanted to stay.

Dick Waterhouse was in the same class. He was a bully, who, if Betty didn't save a sandwich for him to eat on his way home from school, gave her "a really good hiding". When Betty's dad found out — he worked with Dick's father, another telephone engineer in Halifax — he soon put a stop to that.

In 1928 Betty had diphtheria, and was taken to Stoney Royd Isolation Hospital. Her mother and Joan had to go to a relation's home until after the Health Department had fumigated the house. In 1933 Joan became ill with the disease. In the bedroom at Trough Farm, where Joan lay ill, was a wooden wash-stand with a marble top. On it stood a big jug patterned with roses and butterflies. Beneath the bed was a matching chamber pot.

Joan was delirious, her visions taking even more terrifying forms than the ghost stories Betty used to spin for her. Behind the wash-stand loomed a tall white figure, heading towards her bed. She had a dangerously high temperature, and went to Northowram Isolation Hospital.

Every patient was given a number, and progress of the illness was monitored in the local newspaper. "Comfortable", "serious" or "dangerously ill" was published against each number. When the paper arrived in the evening, it was an important moment for those who had relations in isolation hospitals. When the majority of homes did not own a telephone, that was their means of finding out the condition of the patient. But they weren't to know about "illness lice", as Joan described them. All the children's heads had to be swathed in a white cloth with something applied on them to kill any lice. They were kept on for a day, then the hair was washed. Betty was identified as being a carrier of the diphtheria germ.

After Wainstall's Infant School, the children went to Haugh Shaw School at Savile Park. At eleven, Betty went to the swimming baths with the school. The teacher, Miss Normington, was amazed on ordering the children to get into the water, when Betty dived in expertly and swam to the side. She had already had lessons from the Sunday school teacher, at 3s for twelve lessons, plus 1d each time for entry to the baths.

When twelve, Betty embarked on sewing lessons at school. Her teacher was Miss Elsie Pollard. Scholars were asked to take an old garment to fashion another "new" one for themselves. Betty took a discarded dress of her Grandma's. With the teacher's help the dress took shape. Many schools were assisting scholars to be thrifty in similar manner. "Waste not, want not" was a maxim usefully followed both then and during the war. The outcome was that Betty, in her renewed dress, took part in a kind of mannequin parade at the Marborough Hall in Halifax. Selected girls in their home-made outfits paraded round the large hall, to the background music of *In a Country Garden*. A notice pinned to the material on the top of her dress announced, "Made from Grandma's old dress".

CHAPTER
TWELVE

Eleanor

"I shall get up and I shall scream!" was the defiant first recollection of Eleanor May Buckley's childhood. Her mother smacked her and sent her back to bed. Not an auspicious beginning to life. With her parents, Sarah and Edward, Eleanor lived in a terraced house at 44, Colnebridge Road, Bradley, for her first years.

Next-door neighbour Mrs Carpenter used to call the little girl into her home. "Take me clogs off, rub me feet, and sing to me, Eleanor." Mrs Carpenter's legs were encased in thick lisle stockings which formed wrinkles like concertinas all the way down to her ankles. The song the child sang never varied. It was *Home on the Range*.

The cinema, and cowboy films, were becoming part and parcel of everyday life, even in Colnebridge, where there was little chance of buffalo, deer or antelopes playing as in the cowboy song. Nor was it where the other words of *Home on the Range* applied either: "Where seldom is heard, a discouraging word, and the skies are not cloudy all day." But no wonder everyone loved to sing; there were such happy, tuneful songs coming out of "Tin Pan Alley" during the 1920s and 1930s.

In the "Tin Mission" at Bradley, a Methodist chapel so called because of its corrugated tin type of construction, sober hymns were sung. There was a small platform for the choir, and for when five-year-old Eleanor sang a solo one Whitsuntide: *In Our Dear Lord's Garden*. She adored her new white silk dress, with a cape that softly brushed against her bare arms that glorious summer Sunday afternoon.

It was the best time of year, with only a few weeks to go before Huddersfield Holiday Week, at the beginning of August, when the family went either to Blackpool or Scarborough, though they did try Rhyl one year.

What a palaver it was, packing. Although men usually buy special clothes for summer, Edward never even had a short-sleeved shirt, and just rolled his ordinary shirt sleeves up if it was extra warm. A pair of "flannel bags" (trousers) saw him through the summer. They always took mackintoshes, just in case, and, of course, Eleanor's swimming costume. It was cheaper "keeping yourself" in a boarding house, so tins of food were packed into the already weighty case. Edward needed a week's holiday to recuperate after carrying that dead weight to the station. Eleanor's contribution to preparations was to sit on top of the case while her mother tried to lock it. If one side seemed to be locked, it suddenly sprang open again as the other lock was being attended to. It isn't always an advantage to be thin. Someone fat sitting on top of the case would have been far better, and squashed the contents together sooner. Carrying that case was the worst part of the holiday, with Edward almost wishing the week was over, the tins of food consumed, and they were on the way home again, and it would be another year before it all had to be gone through again. The return journey was never as onerous for him as it was for Eleanor and her mother, taking one last look at the sea for as long as they possibly could.

Eleanor had no need to scream for a new bucket and spade to make sand castles. It was the very first thing they bought once the case had been unpacked. A few red, white and blue paper flags were also bought to stick on top of the sand castles, and Dad enjoyed making a moat and a gulley reaching to the sea.

At Rhyl there was a large tiered wooden stand on the sands for holidaymakers to sit on while listening to the Salvation Army band singing hymns and banging tambourines. The navy and red uniforms were so attractive, especially the lady members' bonnets, tied with big bows beneath their chins. At first crowds were drawn by them singing "I think I am, I know I am, I'm H-A-P-P-Y", spelling out the last word. "Go and join in," Mrs Buckley urged her small daughter, Mrs Carpenter of Colnebridge's singing star. But Eleanor drew the line at singing in public on the sands at Rhyl.

More often, Huddersfield Holiday Week was spent in Blackpool. But there was no money to spend on shows or the Tower circus. It was enough to have been able to manage a week at the seaside. Besides, lots of entertainments were free. What was more entertaining than simply watching other people? Or going into one of the arcades where Feldman's sheet music publishers had a piano and someone singing the latest hit song in an attempt to promote sales. The music usually cost 6*d* a copy and with a few of those they could have a marvellous sing-song round the piano back at "the digs".

Eleanor went to bed at eight, and her parents then either played cards in the front room of the boarding house or joined in the merry sing-songs with the other guests. About nine, Edward and a few of the men went out for a drink, and it *was* only one.

When people went to Blackpool for Huddersfield Holiday Week they could be certain of meeting others they knew from their home town, Blackpool being the most popular resort for Northerners to converge on during the 1920s and 1930s — "A home from home" as some scribbled on the backs of comic postcards to their friends and relations. "Hello, fancy seeing you here!" could be heard all over, and arms were linked and they all started singing up the promenade, "Oh, I do like to be beside the seaside, Oh I do like to be beside the sea."

Well-known faces, often from the same street, loomed up on piers, the pleasure beach, all over. Blackpool seemed to be swarming with just about everybody they knew, as if everyone from Huddersfield had migrated there for that one heady week in August. Indeed, at Mrs Moore's boarding house, two more families had arrived from Leeds Road, where the Buckleys then lived. One of the families also had an aspiring songstress, aged ten. Her party piece, when the sing-song was going strong round the piano, was *It's a Sin To Tell a Lie*, followed by *Red Sails In the Sunset*.

Mrs Moore ran the boarding house single-handed, and the day began by heaving great big jugs full of hot water up the stairs into each family room. Guests provided their own soap and towels, which, when wet, were hung out of the bedroom window, the sash being brought down to make sure the towels didn't drop onto the roofs below.

After one person had washed with some of the hot water in the pottery bowl which stood on the marble-topped wooden furniture, it was poured into a bucket then some measured out for the next. It was harder trying to gauge when one of the lavatories on the landings would be vacant. Sometimes, despairing of the "Engaged" sign changing to "Vacant", guests went outside in search of a public toilet on the promenade. And how embarrassing if someone had forgotten to push the bolt on, momentarily thinking they were at home and it didn't matter who barged in.

The Buckleys had their cooked meal at midday. Sauce bottles were prominent on each table. But before any sands could be gone to, shopping had to be attended to, buying meat, fish or whatever it was they decided upon at local shops. But even that was part of the holiday ritual, and it was interesting going into new shops, and tasting different food. How luxurious to be able to read the paper, or do a bit of knitting sitting on deckchairs while Mrs Moore did the cooking! Teas were simple. Jam and bread, finishing with tinned fruit and a bun each. It was always tea to drink, never coffee.

A family could gauge how long it had been since anyone else had stayed in their room by the date on the newspapers lining the chest of drawers. Reading them was something to do occasionally while waiting for the rain to stop. Even if there was rain, it dried quicker at Blackpool, and the sun bravely came out as though it didn't dare do anything else, it being the annual week's holiday.

Eleanor had a ball and a story book bought while in Blackpool. Her parents were keen to encourage their daughter to read. Holidays were from Saturday to Saturday. Neighbours bought any bread, meat or other necessity for the Sunday, and asked the milkman to leave a bottle on the Sunday morning, with a saucer to protect it from marauding birds or animals until the holidaymakers arrived home.

One of the Buckley's neighbours saved all her empty jam jars for the week after her seaside week. Employers didn't give holiday pay, so, after the extravagance of a week at Blackpool, some means had to be thought up to get through the following week. The lady made lots of preserves, lemon cheese and so on, and she therefore had saved quite a lot of jars. She could take them to the grocer, who paid 2d on each 2 lb jar, and 1d for 1 lb jars. This meant that she could buy groceries to live on until she had a week's pay for working again.

Dismay at the holiday being over soon vanished at the sight of schoolfriends again, and playing out.

Mrs Buckley, when "feeling flush", gave herself and Eleanor a treat, by going to *two* cinemas on a Saturday afternoon. These were either the Grand or the Tudor, with a pennyworth of ice cream in a glass for Eleanor at Coletta's in the Market Hall in between the pictures, and two pennyworth for Sarah. What a treat! They liked Ginger Rogers and Fred Astaire films best. Eleanor was absolutely dazzled by the glamorous clothes they wore, the evening dresses, black tails and top hats. Then there was the Pathé news, which began with that crowing cockerel. How amazing to actually see on the news famous people walking about, instead of just flat and still in a newspaper. Eleanor loved to see Princess Elizabeth and Princess Margaret Rose, or Shirley Temple on the news.

On Christmas Eve she and her mother went on a bus to Sheffield, to spend Christmas with Grandma and Grandad. Edward following on a later bus after finishing work at ICI. There weren't any toys there, but Grandma let Eleanor play with her brass scales and weights. Her mother didn't allow her to do anything like that. At night time a stocking was hung up. On Christmas Day morning it contained a spice pig with curly string tail, an apple and an orange, and a few shiny pennies. How entertaining it was when the kitchen table was cleared, to spin those pennies and see how many stayed spinning before dropping. Eleanor had a new doll as well, but that never fitted in the stocking. Her favourite doll had a porcelain head and papier-maché body. She helped Grandma, who spent most of the morning making apple and mustard sauce to go with the pork, and peeling the potatoes and vegetables.

One year a brother arrived, Alan, who made a far better playmate than either her doll or Grandma's weigh scales. A few years younger than Eleanor, she enjoyed helping to look after him, and being able to read bedtime stories to him. And when Huddersfield Holiday Week came round again, she would be able to teach him the ins and outs of making sand castles and moats at Blackpool.

CHAPTER
THIRTEEN

The Boat Makers

When you've got a best friend, you can face anything. Maynard Mortimer and Geoffrey Wilson were that kind of chums in the 1930s. One day, during a school holiday, Maynard observed to Geoffrey, "There's a pot of gold at the end of that rainbow, let's go and find it." It was as good a way of spending a boyhood day as any.

The pair walked and walked, trudging manfully on in their quest, but never seeming to get any nearer. A thunderstorm broke, and their clothes became sodden through when they arrived in Kirkheaton. All they received for their trouble was a "good hiding".

Intermittently they had strokes of fortune. A boy was needed to push a "Stop Me And Buy One" Wall's ice-cream cart in the school holidays. It wasn't the pot of gold they had longed to find at the end of the rainbow, but 18s was a sizeable sum and not to be sniffed at.

In 1939 the two pals had a craze for making rafts. The river Colne at the back of ICI seemed to them wasted with no shipping on it. Maynard then had a better idea. "Why don't we make a canoe?" They set to work at once, fired with each other's enthusiasm, pinching pieces of wood from Maynard's home in Glenfield Avenue, and borrowing a book from the school library called *How To Make A Boat*. Part of an old bed came in useful. Air-raid pegs were used for ribs, and plenty of nails lying about came in handy. A car belonging to one of the boy's dads had been laid up in the garage. It had tarpaulin over it. Maynard and Geoffrey considered a better use could be made of it, so they tacked it over the "canoe". A can of paint was also purloined. After all, it was in a good cause. They may become famous boat-builders.

The canoe finished, the boys ran all the way home from school. They couldn't wait to try it out. It was never launched. Maynard's dad stormed out of the house, making them pull all the nails out, before smashing it up and setting fire to it. Talk about dreams going up in smoke!

Another *Boy's Own*-type adventure beckoned not long afterwards: biking and camping at Bridlington. There were a few ramshackle bell tents and caravans. Maynard and Geoffrey found "a lovely piece of grass" and erected their tent on it. A burly fellow bore down on them, seething with wrath. The "stupid fools" had erected it in the gangway. They had to tear it down immediately. On they went to Flamborough, and had another attempt at putting up the tent — and ended up being stranded on the cliffs. Somebody told them they'd have to stay there until the tide went out. The lads, undeterred, climbed up the steep and tortuous Flamborough cliffs, went to a café and wanted to know "What can you give us for sixpence?" Geoffrey has been back to the scene since, and will never know how they climbed to the top of those cliffs. Maybe having the moral support of a Best Friend did the trick.

But even having a best friend was of little use when, after some misdemeanour, butcher Sheard hung one of the boys up by his jacket collar on a meat hook in his shop window, in between a side of beef and a string of sausages.

CHAPTER
FOURTEEN

Special Days

Special Days, such as Easter, Whitsuntide, Summer Holidays and Christmas, divide the year. But there used to be special days for special activities every week. Monday was cold meat, chips and pickles day, an easy meal when washing was on the go. Or mashed-up turnip, carrots and potatoes fried with onions. Tuesday after school, when at Greenhead High School, was for meeting Mother at Rushworth's corner, and tea in the Kingsway Café down King Street, anxiously wondering if I'd have time to attend to the homework in my bulging satchel after going to the Palace with our shop's free pass. Wednesday was half-day closing. During school holidays we often "had a jaunt out" as dad phrased it. Perhaps a bus trip to Harrogate to visit Uncle Willie, or the magical Mother Shipton's cave at Knaresborough, where astounded visitors threw gloves or other odds and ends into the water which eventually turned them to stone. Thursday was Mending Day, when Dad's cousin Annie came to help out with the mending. Darning socks, with them spread over the wooden "mushroom". The darn was practically invisible after her attentions, whereas Mother, who had absolutely no patience at all with such mundane tasks, left a heel looking infinitely worse than when she began. On Friday mornings mob-capped Mrs Hudson came in to blacklead the Yorkshire range and clean the cutlery. There was a big round wooden contraption where knives, spoons and forks were pushed it for some kind of special attention. Newspapers were spread over the wooden table, along with an imposing array of cleaning fluids, soft rags and new yellow dusters. When not at school I enjoyed helping Mrs Hudson. How exciting polishing the cutlery until you could see your face in it, long and thin in the knives, a bit like Stan Laurel, and upside-down in the scooped-out part of the spoons. Mrs Hudson's face looked best in the teapot, it being too ample a face to get it all into a knife or even a dessert spoon.

Every Monday morning at school, assembly began with the hymn "When morning gilds the sky, my heart awaking cries, may Jesus Christ be praised". Or occasionally headmaster Oliver Smith decided to have "Let all the world, in every corner sing, my God and King". Collop Monday was a day to think pleasurably about when horrible sums followed assembly. Oh, roll on big school clock to twelve, when substantial oval collops, edged with crispy fried bits, seasoned with salt, pepper and vinegar filled my plate. Woe betide Mother if she forgot what day it was.

And the pleasure of Pancake Tuesday, Shrovetide as it used to be called. The worst of winter behind, with lighter evenings and playing out ahead, and pancakes, piles of them, with Mother trying hard to toss them high in the air without them falling onto the rug for the cats to leap on. Watching her was half the fun.

Lightly browned, sprinkled with sugar, fingers sticky with oceans of lemon juice — divine! But pancakes on any other day would not taste the same.

Once a month, Dad's ancient Aunt Emma and daughter Winnie paid a duty visit. The sight of Aunt Emma through the little window wc could look through from the back room to see what customer was in the shop, sent Mother flying upstairs out of the way. Emma, with her floor-sweeping black dress, coat and bonnet, and tawny-coloured "I'm sure it's a wig" hair, sank onto the black horsehair sofa, while Winnie, who never uttered a word, just gazed out of the kitchen window. Mother ran the bath water, hoping they'd have gone, or taken the hint, by the time the mythical bath was over. Dad had to take over handing out tea and biscuits and bringing them up to date with the latest family gossip.

One of my favourite Special Days as a child in the 1930s while still at the council school before passing the 11-plus and graduating to Greenhead High School, was of being away from school ill. Having a sore throat was enough to warrant a note being given to a schoolchild who came into the shop for sweets on the way up to school, to give to Miss Walker.

Until I heard the last child leave the shop, and knew the register was being called and Hazel Taylor wouldn't be there to reply "Here, Miss", I lay doggo. Then, like Lazarus rising from the dead, I gloried in the knowledge that I had all those hours in front of me to do as I pleased. It was specially gratifying if the snow was gently falling past my bedroom window, and instead of me getting cold and wet Mother would be up and downstairs like a yo-yo rubbing my chest with Vick, then pinning a scarf with a safety pin round my shoulders to "keep your little neckhole warm". Hot drinks galore put in an appearance, such as Bovril and Ovaltine. If it was Horlicks it was sent back from whence it came, despite protestations of, "But it will do you good." How can something you hate do you any good?

Alone at last, I was free to pursue the main object of my Special Day. In a bookcase, I'd come across a sizeable glass dome with a likeness of Blackpool Tower and promenade inside. The back was sealed with white paper, like that used to wrap customers' bread in. If I could scratch that off, bit by laborious bit, and if I concentrated really hard, it was all I needed to do to get into Blackpool by that secret, back entrance. If I kept at it, despite having to keep stopping to put my hands on the hot-water bottle because they kept getting so cold, I could have walked on the prom and back, and be in bed again by dinnertime. What a diverting morning I spent! There'd be no need for trains. Blackpool was there in front of me and how much more entertaining it was than repeating multiplication tables.

But by the time the bowl of brown Windsor soup and another hot-water bottle were brought up, Blackpool and the somewhat wild idea of getting inside that dome was still as far away as ever, which was probably just as well. Eventually I tired of the project and gave up the ghost, so to speak, of spending a morning by the sea by sheer will power alone.

Reading film star annuals and my hefty Grimms' book of fairy tales was a bit of a problem in an unheated bedroom, especially when snow was piling thicker and higher on the window outside. I always thought, "What if it never stops, what if it goes on falling forever?", which by some fluke of nature I supposed it could.

My hands became numb with cold, propped-up pillows slithered annoyingly down, and medicine three times a day and a screwed-up face each time eventually took the pleasure out of an unofficial day from school. Occasionally sleep overcame me, and I awoke with a shock to realize the shades of evening were already drawing in on a December afternoon, and where had the missing hours gone to?

Comics like *Tiger Tim, Funny Wonder* and *Chips* had slithered off the eiderdown. A creaking floorboard on the staircase and stealthy footsteps announced that Mother was creeping up quietly in case I was asleep. If I wasn't, and the stealth had all been in vain, she burst into song, perhaps "Hush, hush, hush, here comes the Bogey Man" complete with exaggerated actions. She quite enjoyed "having somebody to see to", as long as the illness wasn't serious and likely to be prolonged.

An ardent fan of the old time music hall songs, she enacted them as good as any star of those days. We'd have *Soldiers of the Queen* marching and saluting to an imaginary superior across the linoleum-covered bedroom floor, perhaps with one of the cats in her arms as a subaltern, then *Burlington Bertie, Two Lovely Black Eyes* and *Have You Ever Been Lonely, Have You Ever Been Blue?* There was no wireless or television in a 1930s bedroom, but what a terrific floor show! She was superb enacting *The Man on the Flying Trapeze,* swooping all over the place. Her vitality was far more infectious than any sore throat. Then my teddy bear was waltzed round to *Daddy Wouldn't Buy Me a Bow-Wow, Bow-Wow,* and if Prince was having a look to see when I was getting up, he'd be swooped up onto his hind legs as a willing dancing partner. How glad I was that my mother's recipe for an invalid was acting the giddy goat, and that she didn't believe in walking around with a long face.

And for tea, what more suitable for a convalescing schoolchild than a freshly laid egg from one of our hens in the henyard round the back, with a slice or two of thinly-cut Hovis, Turog or Bermaline bread cut lengthways into "soldiers" to dip into the runny yolk. No other way would do.

Being ill, if only for a day, brings to mind Funeral Teas. An air of dignity and gloom, so unlike normal days at our shop, took over. Even the cats and Prince took on an expression of mourning.

The big kitchen table had two wooden "leaves" inserted by Grandad, turning a handle at one end of the table where there was a hole to fit it into. In our childhood days my brother Philip and I gloried in being allowed to sit at either end of the table and watch the distance between us disappear as the gap widened. The boards, kept behind the cellar door, seemed ideal for bearing a corpse themselves.

If at school, how I hoped the tea would be in progress on my return. Mourners in floor-length black — older ladies tended to keep the long dresses even when more emancipated women wore shorter ones — all suitably ashen faced, one or two with pink edging round their eyes, small with crying. Gentlemen didn't seem to cry, but their pale jaws clenched and unclenched with unreleased emotion. The ladies kept their hats on, perhaps thinking if they removed them it may be their turn next. There was no chance of being laid out as long as your hat was still in place.

Gentlemen were impeccably dressed in black striped trousers and plain black jackets, or dark overcoats often with velvet collars if the funeral tea took place in winter. Then, those seated at the side of the table near to the blazing coal fire were frequently in some danger of cremation. What an impressive scene it made, like so many tall, upright, black beetles waiting for the feast to commence.

Tiny pots of freshly-made Colman's mustard with adorable miniature spoons were placed at intervals down the stiffly-starched white cloth. Cruet sets in cut glass were placed at both ends of the table. There were ham and hard-boiled egg sandwiches, with garnishings of mustard and cress or parsley, and three-tiered silver cake stands, each with a fancy white paper doyley for the sponge sandwiches, macaroons, and iced buns — some with pink icing in an attempt to jolly up the mourners — with half a glacé cherry on top of each.

I do believe that my appearance provided a new dimension to the mourners' thoughts, as I quietly pulled up a buffet, casting grieving minds back to their own faraway schooldays. Meanwhile, I couldn't imagine how it must feel to suddenly be plunged into complete, damp, earthy darkness and to miss having tea, and not only that day's tea, but all the other teas for all eternity.

To hear the conversation, one could be forgiven for imagining that a saint had just been laid to rest. One advantage of dying is that all at once, all the bad points of a person's character are seemingly forgotten and obliterated at one fell swoop.

A wasp or hungry fly could disorganize even the most orderly of occasions in summer. And how riveted my eyes were to the long, sticky, beige-yellow fly-catcher, swaying in the breeze above the table, with its victims in their death throes, an ever-present reminder of life and mortality. How I loved it all!

Maytime, with bluebells, sandals with little holes punched in the fronts, short white tennis socks, and, on 12 May 1937, when I was ten, the magnificent Coronation of King George VI and Queen Elizabeth. The scandal of Edward and Mrs Simpson was already receding into history.

A favourite pastime was cutting out pictures of the two princesses, Elizabeth and Margaret Rose, and sticking them into big scrapbooks with flour and water paste. What fascinated me most about the Coronation was that now, Princess Elizabeth, only a year older than

I was, would one day be Queen of England. The wireless, papers and magazines were full of features about them, especially about Elizabeth, heiress presumptive to the throne.

Constantly, I tried to imagine what they were doing in Buckingham Palace. Say on a Friday evening, when my friends and I had climbed up onto the "ack" (the sloping tiled roof of the low-decker opposite our shop) to have caterpillar races. We kept them in matchboxes with air holes punched in them, with a bed of cabbage or lettuce for them to gather their strength before The Big Race.

The starting point was the end of the roof. Unwilling, lazy "woolly boys" were given an unceremonious push with a matchstick, to make them undulate competitively to the winning post, up at the top. On summer evenings, when doors were open, we could occasionally hear the strains of Henry Hall's Dance Band, or that of Jack Payne, playing *Red Sails in The Sunset, Happy Days Are Here Again* and *Here's to the Next Time*. One thing was sure about the new heiress to the throne's activities — she wouldn't be having a caterpillar race on the roof of Buckingham Palace.

Coronation mugs and other souvenirs filled the shops. Every baby in the Municipal Maternity Home in Greenhead Road received a Coronation spoon. Authorized expenditure of Huddersfield Corporation on local celebrations was £3,500. A gift for each schoolchild was valued at 1s. Boys over eleven received a Coronation pocket penknife, girls over eleven a spoon of better quality than those younger. Under elevens were presented with a book, *Our King and Queen*, published by Oxford University Press.

On the day before the Coronation, on the afternoon of 11 May, children were presented with the souvenirs. Mothers of children under five were asked to take them to schools during the afternoon.

There was great rejoicing on the 12th, much of it for the fact that schools had closed until the 24th. Children in Dock Street, Castlegate, enjoyed a tea and Carnival on the big day itself, and the mayor, Councillor Joseph Barlow, attended.

The climax locally of the day was a Grand Coronation Dance in the Town Hall, with music provided by Roland Powell's Rhythm Kings. Tickets were 2s, and proceeds were given to local charities.

Those of us too young to attend dances enjoyed ourselves dressing up as kings and queens, and having pretend coronations. Our thrones were tree stumps or upturned buckets, old sheets made adequate robes to parade round back gardens in, and cake tins with bits of gold and silver paper from bars of chocolate stuck on made impressive crowns. A child with a mouth organ had practised playing *God Save Our Gracious King* and I'm sure it sent shivers down the spines of the locally elected new king and queen. All I wanted to be was Princess Elizabeth.

Every child needs an idol to look up to. Who better than Princess Elizabeth, our future queen? The epitome of politeness, graciousness, and a role model for children of the 1930s, she was always so smartly dressed too. But even the poorest of children did their

95

utmost to make the best of what rags and tatters they possessed. As mothers always said, "There's no disgrace in being poor, as long as you make the best of what you have, and who you are."

CHAPTER
FIFTEEN

Alec

The effects of the First World War reached far into the future, determining the lives of yet unborn children. Alec, born in 1927, feels compassion for the father who left his mother destitute, with nine children to rear alone. His father fought in the war, a 6 ft tall, broad-shouldered, intelligent youth of eighteen when he joined up. Two years later he returned, totally paralysed down the left side, and with a steel plate in his head, suffering, as many others did, the agony of shell shock. Memories of being shelled, day after day.

Back home in England his only income was the £2 a week awarded the totally disabled. He met and married a lady who already had two children. Despite inauspicious prospects, the couple produced another eight. Their maternal grandparents, despite having brought up a family of ten themselves, took the eldest girl to be brought up with them.

Even in the 1920s, a family of ten children was considered quite large. Alec recalls his father's perpetual restlessness, always wanting to be on the move to somewhere else, continually moving to first one ramshackle old house then another. But at that time families rented homes, and didn't have a mortgage, so moving was easier. Rents were only a few shillings a week, but with only £2 a week to live on they weren't in a position to pick and choose. Some places were almost unfit for human habitation.

But children tend to be resilient, and to treat each day as a new adventure. That's how Alec looked at it. He was excited at the prospect of moving again, every time it was suggested. He had no qualms or distress, even though on the night prior to "flitting", as it used to be termed in Yorkshire, parents and children slept on the floor, as the beds had to be dismantled. They had to be off first thing next morning. Bed springs had long since lost their spring, so strong rope was used to support the mattresses. The children called them "ropey beds".

Two or three children shared each bed when not on the move, which was very comforting on dark cold nights. On the most severe winter nights each bed was allowed one hot oven shelf, wrapped in a piece of flannelette sheet. Battle commenced when three pairs of feet in each bed fought for the warmest spot.

In Yorkshire, real, old-fashioned winters with snow drifting in feet, not just inches, were normal in the 1920s and 1930s. It was a struggle simply to survive, but it tested the ingenuity of the children's mother greatly, and resulted in the introduction of novel ideas. They could have as much bran as they wanted, given by a farmer. Before the children set off for school, dry bran was poured into their boots, providing a warm insole and keeping their feet dry on the walk to school.

Sheets of thick brown paper were cut into "leggings" and tied round legs. Old socks substituted for gloves. Hand-knitted scarves were wound round the chest more than once then tied at the back with a safety pin. Country people set great store on keeping the chest warm.

As the oldest children grew out of their clothes, garments were passed down to the younger ones. Sou'westers, with elastic beneath the chin, afforded protection against driving wind, rain and snow. Poor Alec was mortified when he lost his in a snowdrift, another child having pulled it off his head "for a joke".

It was cheaper to buy potatoes by the sack loads, and they were ranged round the kitchen wall. It was too cold to store them outside. In any case, they helped keep draughts out. Ernie, the eldest boy, often had to walk across the snow-covered moors of North Yorkshire to buy a stone of flour. Many anxious moments were experienced until he returned. It was a round journey of some four miles, and it was not unknown for walkers to be caught up in a blinding white blizzard, perishing in an attempt to find the way home, but there was never enough money to buy in advance.

One move was to Castleton, where the rovers settled into a large old mill house, surrounded by fields, with a river alongside, the water being used to drive the huge mill wheel. Ironically, the house was occupied by "gentry" at one time, and there were still servants' bells and a huge drive leading to some stables. There were still some paintings adorning the walls even then, in 1932.

The initial delight of living by a river soon spelt near disaster after a lengthy period of torrential rain. As the river swelled to a dangerous level, the family were sitting round the kitchen table eating their last cooked meal for several days. Alec's father, reminded of his army life in the trenches, with the water in them frequently waist high, took command. "Keep calm, keep calm, pick up your plates and go upstairs to the large room at the far side of the house." All eyes had turned towards the kitchen door, where initially the water was only a trickle, but was soon flooding the uneven stone floor. The room upstairs had been prepared, with food stored and bottles of water. How fortunate that every one of the children always did exactly what they were told to do, and despite lack of material goods were well schooled in obedience. They were cut off for five days, with water surrounding the house to a depth of five or six feet.

That was enough of *that* place. Another move was called for. On to Staithes, near Whitby, renting an old house near the harbour. Rents were much dearer there, and probably the catalyst of ensuing disasters. One of Alec's sisters, quaintly named Winsome, two years older than he, died from pneumonia. His mother was distraught. Six of the other children had measles, and when the doctor arrived at last it was too late. Alec's father borrowed a dark overcoat for the funeral, and the child was buried near Staithes.

Rent was owing, and there was no money to pay it with. Another baby was on the way. There was some talk about them all camping out in an ex-Army tent, until, as Mr Micawber was wont to say, "something turns up". What did turn up was a move to the workhouse, and Alec's father went back to live with his mother "until things straightened out" and he found another house. The workhouse, to Alec, was merely another halting place in a succession of adventures. In his child's eyes, the huge stone building that confronted him could have been a palace. It seemed to have hundreds of corridors with rooms leading off them. Young boys were put in a ward to sleep with old men. It was an awful experience to hear his mother crying hysterically when her new-born baby was taken away from her, until communal tea-time when all the mothers of new-born babies had to breast-feed them, quite openly, round the enormous kitchen table.

Thick slices of bread with bright yellow margarine were provided for the children's tea, and sometimes they were given a sort of minced beef with potatoes. Alec doesn't recall having vegetables.

A tough bloke was in charge of the young men, who were segregated. It was a brutal place for them, and every morning they were busily sawing and chopping up logs, as a means of paying for a night's "bed and board". During the night where the boys were in the ward with the old men it resembled Bedlam, with a lot of shouting going on if one of them soiled his bed. Alec thought they must have gone there to die. But there was a bonus being in the workhouse — the clean, white sheets on the beds, instead of old, patched, flannelette ones.

The building was surrounded by tall, spiked, iron railings. The yard where logs were stored was used by the children as a play area. They never went beyond, but could peer through the railings onto the road. Occasionally passers-by handed sweets to the youngsters through the railings. Three months went by, and there was not a sign of Alec's father. Then, out of the blue one morning, all of them were given a hot bath, a railway warrant was handed to their mother, and another big adventure ensued. This was their first ride on a train. Sitting opposite Alec on the two-hour journey was a prisoner, handcuffed to a policeman. At least now Alec was free again. Their father awaited them in a rented house at Eaglescliffe, near Stockton. Many homeless families wandered up and down past the house, aimlessly trying to get through another day. But none of the family liked not living in the country, so a few months later off they went again, ending up in a pretty little village called Langthorne. Again, it was a massive, run-down house, but with walled gardens and even a small orchard. By this time it was 1937, and Alec was ten years old.

The rural, idyllic surroundings were ruined by constant rows between his parents. When not at school, the children were busy gathering sticks in fields and woods to keep the home fires burning. A local farmer had given them permission to gather them. Only rarely could they afford a bit of coal. But life wasn't always a long round of bickering. There were some harmonious moments when mother and father, for a brief time, recaptured whatever had brought them together initially, and they sang duets together. There was no accompaniment of course, not even a piano, but how pleasant it was to hear them singing *Just a Song at Twilight* and *Drink to Me Only With Thine Eyes*. With a couple of ancient oil lamps either side of the flickering wood fire, and "fairies up the chimney" (sparks flying up from the wood) the children were happy for a brief time.

Happiness, however, is a fragile condition, and liable to shatter when least expected. The children were all in bed one night. Their mother entered. "Your father has left us", she informed them starkly, "but I've laid the fires in case any of you are poorly."

So that was it. Rock bottom. Without a father, on public assistance. The First World War had truly stretched its awful heritage across the years, to engulf them all. However, if they had nothing else, each one of them had the support of a large and closely-knit family around them. Even in the workhouse they had never been alone, as some children in Doctor Barnardo's so often were. Others were much worse off. Tramps were numerous, sleeping in the woods, taking their billy cans to house doors, begging for them to be filled with a drink of tea. Alec's mother, even in her dire poverty, always strove to give a slice of bread or plain cake to those destitute mortals.

The family always attended church, walking the few miles there and back twice on Sundays. If the children were alone, their mother at home with the youngest, they sang hymns on the way back to keep their spirits up on dark winter nights along unlit country roads, with bats swooping over their heads.

With faith, the public assistance, and trust in God to pull them through the travails that so often beset them, life gradually became a little better. At least there weren't the constant rows to live with. Not long afterwards, the local squire rode up on a magnificent horse, accompanied by two or three people. He spoke to the mother of the children, who, back in her own family tree on the maternal side, could trace herself to the French aristocracy. "The vicar has been in touch with me, and alerted me to your plight. We are going to give you five shillings' worth of groceries every week."

Such a gesture almost caused more tears than those that had fallen before, as sometimes an unexpected kindness can do. Squire Stirling Stuart "was a real gentleman", and true to his word the weekly groceries were delivered by another good man, the village grocer, who never forgot to pop in a bag of toffees for the children.

From that moment, though long hard years of struggle still lay ahead, hope, optimism, and, yes, happiness and laughter filled the home. No more quarrelling to endure. They often drank from jam jars, but "if I was very good I got the one with the golliwog on," Alec laughs. Many children would surely envy them, living in such a glorious, unspoilt village, with caring, supportive villagers all around them. They ran freely on the moors in summer as no seaside holidays could be afforded, but what they had never had, as the old adage goes, they never missed. Empty jam jars were taken on the moors to catch bees in, snapping the lids tight as they plundered the clover. Eldest brother Ernie had made some beautiful mud beehives, and had visions of making honey and turning the hobby into a thriving business.

The only Grandad they knew, their mother's father, sent a 15s postal order every Christmas. If it was late, there was a bit of a panic. It didn't seem much, but the grandparents had spent their lives bringing up their own large family, besides taking in their eldest daughter's first child. An auntie sent big parcels of perfectly good clothes that their cousins had no further use for. Their mother made lots of herb beer. Occasionally in the dead of night they'd have a fright when a cork popped with all the pent-up fizz. What heaven on a beautiful summer day in the school holidays to fill empty medicine bottles with herb beer and go out into the wide open spaces. Bags of fresh air, basic food but good. Alec didn't think of that as being deprived, not he! A farmer had given them a few hens, so eggs were plentiful. They were given as much bran as they wanted, the boys caught rabbits, and they had many rabbit pies. They were invited to take basins and catch the blood when a pig was killed, which their mother made black puddings from. Mindful that boys do not live by work alone, the old farmer asked "Does tha want a football?" and forthwith took the bladder straight from the newly deceased pig, blew it up with his mouth, tied it with string, and chucked the new football to them. It didn't last very long, but it was fun while it did.

Every Sunday Alec's mother contrived to prepare a "proper" Sunday dinner for them, with light-as-air Yorkshire puddings, vegetables from the garden or what a farmer gave them, and a bit of beef each. Their mother had been a cordon bleu cook in her earlier years, and could make a tasty meal out of "something and nothing".

The floors were stone, so they didn't need a vacuum cleaner. The girls enjoyed making pegged rugs when the handed down clothes were too small for any of them, yet too good to throw away.

What a treat if they were allowed to have a candle lit on dark winter nights, and all sit round the table on the old Bentwood upright chairs to read by its light. A good education, and being able to amuse themselves, was a priority with their mother, coupled with exemplary behaviour and good manners to everyone they encountered. They may have been without much in the way of material goods, but in what really matters they put many "spoiled rich brats" to shame. Always willing to help, always a pleasant smile for everyone.

There were so many incidents to recall and, in retrospect, to laugh about. All the places they had lived in, such as the row of seven old cottages all full of "weird people", including "Old Mink", as the boys nicknamed him, his nose looking like it was rotting away. Another family were known as "The Dafties". They had two children whose hobby was setting the heather on the moors alight. Then there was the time they were snowed up, back in 1933, and Ernie, being the eldest, pushed open a bedroom window and slid down the drainpipe to dig them out.

When Christmas came round in the village where they settled, a huge "Charity Stocking" was brought to their door. Their mother handed out to each of her children the toy, book, or game most suitable for them. The squire gave a party, and how well dressed he looked in tweeds. Each child who attended was given a whole shilling. Such riches had never been known before. "Taty Picking Week" in September earned the boys 6d a day and a free bucket of "spuds" each. One summer school holiday the farmer next door asked the three older boys to clear his two or three acre field of the yellow weed, ragwort. With old socks to protect their hands, it took the boys the best part of the six weeks, doing other jobs as well in between. All they received was 10s between them.

The boys never moaned about not having money to buy things with. They made whatever they wanted themselves, from whatever came to hand. Sledges were made out of pieces of wood, complete with the irons from a discarded pram chassis. Villagers were only too pleased to have someone take articles that were of no further use.

Meanwhile, their mother was busy doing her utmost to create a happy home. Once she came across some linoleum in a junk shop that was "going for a song". The boys were sent with their home-made "bogey carts" to transport it the four or five miles. On another expedition she bought a spinette "for a quid", Alec recalls in amazement. And it was commonplace for them to sit on Sheraton chairs, as in the 1930s many people were getting rid of "old-fashioned stuff", and simply throwing them out.

Unexpected expenditure could be a worry. Every year a photographer went round the schools and the photographs were sent to parents. Each one cost 6d. With nine children is was a large financial outlay so, reluctantly, the only record of the children's faces in childhood had to be sent back. However, one was always kept of one of the children, and they took it in turns. Alec's turn to keep his photograph was in 1938.

The local Hunt was a marvellous sight for the villagers. All the local gentry assembled at the hall in Crakehall. Alec saw many kills, and blooding the face of the youngest member of the Hunt. Daubed with blood from the carcass of the fox. Then the cubs were dug out and savaged by the hounds.

Alec doesn't remember seeing a tablecloth on the table, only newspapers. His mother baked white bread, never omitting to make a big cross on the loaves "to keep the Devil out of the bread". Breakfast was unleavened bread, and the children stuck their thumbs in to make a "well" for the treacle, so it didn't trickle away.

None of the children had birthday parties. They were simply wished "Many Happy Returns". When Alec had his fourteenth birthday and his mother was working, she gave him 1s, telling him to buy a pair of socks with it. For the first time in his life he rebelled, and threw it across the room. It went down the back of the mantelpiece and was lost forever. This was as bad a moment as when, years before, he had lost his sou'wester in the snowdrift.

The children may not have been able to have new clothes at Whitsuntide, but on Oak Apple Day every one of them sported a spring of oak in their lapels. At Easter, eggs were hard-boiled and rolled in nettles to colour and pattern them for pace-egging, or rolling them up the hill. They never had chocolate Easter eggs. What they had were better in any case.

Alec was eleven before he heard a wireless for the first time, in 1938. He recalls a programme called *Monday Night at Eight*. He visited his Auntie Hilda and Uncle Joe that summer. They took him to the theatre to see *Young Woodley*. This was another first, Alec never having seen inside a theatre before. He thought it marvellous, and the world felt to be opening up with amazing possibilities. His Auntie and Uncle kept a shop, and never before had he been able to wander at will, choosing what he'd like to eat and drink, without thinking of what it may cost.

Then back to school taking sandwiches and milk for midday. Schoolchildren sat around a stove, which was surrounded by a big fireguard. One boy always had an orange after his sandwiches, with a sugar cube pushed into it to make it taste sweeter. Alec thought he must be rich.

The following year, 1939, when the Second World War began, was the time when life began to look up at long last for Alec. As the time came when each boy was old enough to join up, they each used the one and only decent overcoat to go for their interviews. With men leaving jobs to go to war, more work was available for women. The family moved to Catterick, where Alec's mother had been offered work as a cook for the soldiers. All the soldiers were extremely kind to the family, and careers were opening up for the children as they grew older.

Alec never regrets his childhood experiences. For what achievement is there in having wealth if you have not earned it with the sweat of your brow?

All those children, who survived flood, the workhouse, near destitution and hard work throughout their childhood, became respected, well-liked members of society. Unlike many with riches, none of them ever did anything wrong. Their mother was proud of them all. Ernie became an officer in the Tank Corps, and was killed in action in 1942.

It is not the amount of money in the bank that determines what a person is like, but the character and spirit within. The mother who battled against seemingly unsurmountable odds to keep her family together deserves the plaudits.

So many mothers in the same era felt they could not cope alone if they were left with children. So many youngsters spent their childhood in institutions such as Dr Barnardo's. There is no shame in poverty, and so much to be proud of when children emerge from poverty into polite, decent, self-sufficient adults. How much sweeter the victory when the embattled craft reaches the shore, the battle fought and won, than an easy ride through life.

Alec never for one moment considered his childhood as anything but a Great Adventure, and as for being bore — never. Really, it was marvellous! Though with a few reservations — his mother frequently remarked, "Nobody's up to any good if they aren't in bed by nine o'clock".

CHAPTER
SIXTEEN

Sunday School
Christmas Party

One of the highlights of a schoolchild's year in the thirties was undoubtedly the Sunday School Christmas Party, held a week or so before the great day itself. Children had to take their own food, then pile it onto the table to be shared. Some took jellies, others fish paste sandwiches, and there were lots of bloater sandwiches.

Living at the village shop, Philip, my brother, and I had lots of contributions. We couldn't have been more excited if we'd had an invitation to Buckingham Palace, for Father Christmas himself was going to appear.

Getting ready for the party entailed a skirmish and a few outraged tears beforehand. Why should I have to wear a liberty bodice under a party dress? "You'll get pneumonia if you don't" was the unconvincing reply from Mother. She buttoned me into it, then turned her back to get out the pink satin, frilly party dress. But the offending article had been torn off and flung on the bed. Eventually I was convinced that, it being sleeveless, it wouldn't show. At five years old a girl can be extremely fashion conscious. I bet Shirley Temple and Princess Elizabeth didn't have to undergo the indignity of wearing a liberty bodice at *their* Christmas parties.

But in the days before central heating, and with the door of the Sunday school continually opening, letting in gusts of icy cold air, I was secretly glad to have the bodice, as well as the fluffy angora cardigan, which was dispensed with to show off the dainty cape sleeves as soon as we arrived at the party.

Brown wellingtons, stiff after the walk down the hill in the bitter cold, were a nightmare to yank off. As Mother bent double and pulled energetically, I thought my whole leg would come off as well. Once she pulled so hard that a wellington shot off and hit one of the teachers in the face, and I slithered off the wooden bench to end up on the wooden floor, dazed and humiliated.

Festivities commenced in the big hall of the Sunday school at four o'clock. Oh, how the minutes dragged until it was time to set off. As Mother walked hand in hand with Philip and me down the hill the December sun was already gone, and the night of stars, magic and presents about to begin.

It was a thrill to enter the big hall from the darkness outside, for everyone had a different look about them. Sunday school teachers had Christmassy twinkles in their usually sober eyes, and even bits of tinsel in their hair — definitely attributes that were not there on normal Sundays.

Coloured streamers and Chinese lanterns were swaying from the ceiling, as were scores of balloons, some as fat as footballs, and others like bloated, shiny, pink sausages. From a real fir tree hung shiny glass baubles, fragile and beautiful, and all manner of little novelties, such as wooden reindeer and Santa Claus, Japanese dolls with miniature parasols, and wrapped chocolate novelties. We could see our faces in the glass baubles. Silly faces, with bulging cheeks and flat noses, which were even better than those we saw in the cutlery that Mrs Hudson cleaned on Friday mornings.

Beneath the tree at the entrance to the hall were blue tissue-wrapped presents for boys, and pink ones for girls. At the topmost pinnacle was the glorious silver-dressed fairy, with long, golden hair. I was sure that she was real, and that on normal working days she dwelt with one of the "Higher Ups" in the Sunday school hierarchy, such as Miss Chinn or Superintendent Langley.

Long wooden tables with criss-cross legs underneath were pushed together down the centre of the hall, and covered with starched tableclothes, whiter than white, and so stiff that they bent if touched. Waiting importantly were the thick, white Sunday school cups, saucers and sandwich plates. Food was set out on larger plates, with cakes on three-tier stands at intervals down the tables. Smiles of gratitude from the helpers greeted every shyly preferred bag of sandwiches, biscuits or buns. Each child was relieved to get that bit of the proceedings over with, in case what they had taken didn't come up to the standard of what the others had brought. Scholars took their own knives, forks and spoons, tied with cotton and names scrawled on a bit of paper in case they became lost.

My new silver dancing slippers had flat pom-poms on the fronts and I hardly dare move into the centre of the throng where the big boys pushed and shoved each other, in case one trod on my shoes. Some of the poorer boys had only heavy boots to wear even at a party, and lunged around in a mad fever of gleeful clumsiness. Some mothers didn't give children any dinner if they were going to a party, telling them to "fill their bellies" while there.

Big boys with hungry bellies weren't the only worry. Girls whose parents couldn't afford proper party dresses for them, or soap either, judging by the grimy appearance of their fingernails, were dazzled by silks and satins. Their envy made me feel embarrassed as one or other of them nuzzled against me, grimy fingers lifting satin frills, pawing the dress while I stood frozen with apprehension.

"Aw, ain't it *luvvly*? Can I 'ave it when you've finished with it, eh?"

I said neither yes nor no, and just wished the tea would begin and take the interest onto other things, for I hoped that by summer I'd be able to swank with the dress at weekday school, and not keep it solely for special occasions.

Mother had gone back to the shop, with promises that she would be back when the party was over to walk us safely home. A teacher murmured grace, then helpers bustled about pouring tea from the impressive urns positioned at the top of the tables.

I hoped my brother would sit next to me, but for some reason or other he seemed to want to disown me in public, and was lost to view with his own schoolfriends.

Seeing Grandad's iced buns on the table, some with pink icing, some with white and coconut with half a glacé cherry on top, made me feel self-conscious. It was more interesting — if not dangerous — to eat other people's concoctions, food that looked highly coloured, cheap and slightly evil.

There was usually one infant who had to forego the pleasures of the tea party and be ushered into the cloakroom to be sick, anticipation having proved too much for them. Those of us still upright strained our ears to listen to the awful retchings, which served as an odd accompaniment to the carols being thumped out on the piano.

After tea the tables were removed to make a large area for games. "All make a big, *big* circle for King William," suggested one of the Sunday school teachers. That was my first experience of the stirrings of youthful attraction. I felt I'd die with shame and rejection if Jim, Sam or whoever was standing nonchalantly in the centre chose another girl instead of me. From out the East or West we had all chanted for him to select. Round and round we pounded, booming out, "Down on this carpet you shall kneel, while the grass grows round your feet." Despite the feelings of dismay if we weren't chosen, it was almost worse if we were. How does one kiss anyway? Most times, however, the boys, more embarrassed than the girls, made a lunge for another boy, while onlookers screamed "Cheat, cheat!", and a girl, probably denying her heart's desire, chose her best friend, timidly drawing her back into the middle of the circle.

Cat and Mouse was better. Tension rose to fever pitch as the circle of linked hands, elbows stuck out in all directions to keep out the "cat", protected the "mouse", until the wily cat noticed a break in the link and stormed into the inner circle to grab the shrieking "mouse".

How wonderful it was to have all that length of room to bat balloons about, without constantly banging into furniture or risking the balloon ending up on the fire as in an ordinary home.

Lucy Lockett was enjoyable up to a point, but how I wish they'd provided cushions. Those bare, wooden floorboards were so hard to sit on cross-legged for any length of time. And what about splinters? "Is my dress dirty?" little girls wanted to know, brushing dust from their clean knickers and dresses when the Lucy Lockett game was over. Once the "Drop it, drop it" chant finished as the child on the outside of the circle went round with a handkerchief.

Throughout all the carols, games and jollifications — there were small prizes for those who could say a tongue-twister three times without pausing, or pass an orange beneath the chin to the child on the next seat without dropping it — was the exhilarating knowledge at the back of my mind that somewhere, out in the darkness beyond, Santa Claus and his reindeer were heading in our direction.

Hearts thumped with wild expectation as we grouped round the piano to sing carols, heads swivelling to look at the door at the slightest bump or noise that proclaimed The Arrival. *Good King Wenceslas* was the favourite, and everyone wanted to be the King or Page so they could sing a solo and "Be Important". Runner-up favourites were *While Shepherds Watched Their Flocks By Night* (some of the more unruly elements roared "Washed their socks by night"), *Away In a Manger*, and *I Saw Three Ships Go Sailing By*.

"Please, Miss, is he coming yet?" was the anxiously repeated question as the page was turned for another carol. Then there was a thunderous knocking at the door. I felt quite giddy with delight, yet at the same time a bit apprehensive. The teacher selected a scholar to go and open the door. Quietness descended on the whole room, then in staggered a bent figure in a bright-red cape and tunic, with long, white, wavy beard, thick, curly, white hair, droopy moustache, ruddy cheeks, and twinkling eyes.

"Merry Christmas! Merry Christmas, everyone!" his deep voice boomed. A couple of the youngest children twisted their dresses, sucked their thumbs, and began to cry, but they soon smiled when Santa drew them up to his sack and asked if they liked dollies.

What a huge sack it was, with bumps and strange shapes jutting out all over. Presents were pulled out, and names called.

Little girls accepted shyly and with a polite "Thank you". Some of the big boys quite forgot carefully rehearsed manners and bawled cheekily, "Worrav yer got?" or "Can I have a Meccano set, mister?" or "I want a Dinky car". Pink and blue tissue paper littered the floor, revealing little painting books, crayons, tiny celluloid baby dolls with red-tipped dummies, bath sets for a baby doll, dolls' house furniture and books of dressing dolls. I loved Shirley Temple dressing dolls from Woolworths, with cardboard tabs to hang the dresses over the shoulders.

Pure happiness! When the sack lay limp on the floor Father Christmas took the smallest child on his knee, and sitting on a chair, pulled up to the piano. Now everyone jostled to stand near him, none realizing that the ethereal character was one we saw every Sunday morning in the choir stalls.

Mothers and fathers began to arrive, and the children lined up at the door, boys on one side, girls on the other. Father Christmas gave each one an orange, a new silver threepenny bit and a tangerine before they went out into the frosty air.

The Sunday School Party was over for another year. But before the day was over, Philip and I always knelt at the bedside, or by our mother's knee and closed our eyes to say "The Lord's Prayer", finishing with the words: "And for what we have received, may the Lord make us truly thankful." Then we scrambled into bed to dream of all the fun we'd had at the Sunday School Christmas Party.

CHAPTER
SEVENTEEN

Life Down The Mill Yard

There's a lot to be said for having been born down a mill yard. You tend to be satisfied with your lot, grateful for whatever concessions life occasionally doles out to you.

Granville's dad was an engine tenter and maintenance man in a Colne Valley mill in Linthwaite. He rented a little house in a cobbled yard near the mill. It didn't have an indoor lavatory so the family had to share a row of four wooden holes with wooden slabs to cover them up with. They were out in the yard, and all the mill workers had to pass the house to reach their urgent destination, for the mill had no indoor facilities either. The office lot used to peer out of grimy windows to make sure workers didn't waste too much time chatting or smoking on those "conveniences", and many a raucous quip was shouted from those crossing their legs outside: "Come on, Fred lad, what's tha think tha's doing — making yer will?", or "Na then, Emma lass, get a move on or ah'll come in and give thee a stick o' dynamite."

During the week it was a right carry on attempting to find an empty seat, with mill girls sitting there jawing about Tom, Dick and Harry, and scanning the *Colne Valley Guardian*. Some used to take their own newspapers, a bit too snooty to make do with what the mill provided, stuck on rusty nails hanging on the whitewashed walls. They imagined their own newsprint to be more hygienic, if they ever did consider hygiene.

Granville looked forward to Saturday afternoon and Sundays in the 1930s, when the mill workers were at their own homes. It was sheer heaven to nip in and out of the "lavs" as and when he wanted, without having to trail back because they were full.

The cleansing department men went down the mill yard once a week with a couple of big bins and great whacking shovels to shift the lot. It was a sparse, primitive life. One of the mill workers had too many children and too little wage, half-starving himself to make sure they suffered as little as possible. Granville's mother came to an arrangement with him after finding out that he was "half clammed". Every Friday dinnertime he used to knock at the door, cloth cap respectfully in hand, for his "bit o' rice pudding". She had a huge dish full of rice pudding every Friday, one of those oval enamel dishes with a blue rim round the outside edge. It was enough to feed an army. Fred came for whatever was left over, and after noisily scooping it bone dry, his sleeve was used to wipe any residue off his mouth. "Thanks, missus, that were reet grand." He wasn't seen again near the house until the following Friday.

1933 was a "real" winter of deep snow and hard frosts. What bliss for twins Granville and Margaret to run home from Linthwaite School, and warm frostbitten fingers in the heat of the mill boilerhouse.

For a treat, Granville was allowed to pull the "knocking-off" rope at five o'clock. That operated the mill hooter, a whistle operated by steam. Most of the mill hands were already standing around, on tenterhooks to clock out and shoot off in their clogs to humble cottages, terraced houses and back-to-back homes up the valley. Never to be forgotten was the clatter of their clogs at hometime, a quite different noise of the dragging sound of them going to the mill on a dark winter morning.

After tea in the little house down the mill yard the family settled down to listen to Henry Hall and *We'll All Go Riding on a Rainbow* or Gracie Fields screeching *Sally*, then *The Biggest Aspidistra in the World*, on the wireless set.

Each mill buzzer had a different sound, some high, some low. They sounded in the early morning, for starting work, at midday and at five, and if one howled at any other time it meant fire or some other alarm.

The background music in those days was the constant throbbing of machinery and mill hooters, like the very heartbeat of the West Riding. Gilbert Wheeler looked after one huge engine called "Lizzie", which bore a brass plate with the name on it.

Farmer Jim Cock (how apt a name!) clip-clopped across the cobbled yard with his milk float and horse daily, filling jugs with fresh creamy milk. Some were left outside, little crocheted mats with tiny beads fringing them for a cover if the householder was out. Though often as not the door was left open and the milkman simply walked in.

Wages were low and every penny counted. Granville's complete and utter dismay when going to Linthwaite School in his brand-new cap one winter day is therefore not surprising. His mother's words, ringing in his ears, had been "Now be careful with that cap, money doesn't grow on trees you know." In those days boys had to make their own amusements, and it was quite a long walk up to school. They pinched each other's caps, kicking them like footballs and throwing them around, with the victim a kind of pig in the middle. One boy grabbed Granville's brand-new cap, chucking it high in the air. It landed on a wagon, a moving wagon. The last Granville saw of his new cap was of it sailing away up Manchester Road. He had no appetite for rice pudding or anything else that day. And if he'd had a privy of his own he'd have locked himself in and stayed there until his mother's wrath had worn itself out.

One bath a week, that was the rule. On Friday evenings. The upheaval required for a couple of adults and twins was quite enough to be undertaken only once a week. On other days, Gilbert, back from the mill, had a wash down at the stone sink in the kitchen.

On Fridays the timetable was inviolable. Gilbert was home before the echo of the mill buzzer died away, having only a cobbled yard between him and his work.

After tea, like clockwork, he descended into the cellar, staggering up again with the zinc set pot on his back. The gas ring was lit beneath it, then the tin bath was hauled upstairs.

When the water had boiled, Gilbert and Elsie used buckets and "piggins" to fill the bath while the children played outside, with strict instructions to be back in by half past seven. Elsie put the kitchen clock facing outwards so the twins could see it. In any case, time could be gauged when trains hissed in and out of Golcar Station at regular intervals.

Until bathtime Granville was Tarzan, leaping from wool bale to wool bale with his sister Margaret and their friends. In summertime they lashed a raft together for other adventures, fashioned from old planks and stout rope. The contraption rarely floated, and the River Colne was hardly a compelling waterway for sailing on. It oozed with dye, filth and big rats.

From lighting up the set pot until the water was hot enough took two hours. After filling the two copper kettles and putting them on to heat over the fire, Gilbert ambled across the valley to buy his regular packet of Robin cigarettes from Linthwaite Coop. Those fifty cigarettes had to last the week, and were his only luxury.

Every fortnight on Friday evening he went for a threepenny "short back and sides" at barber Woodruff's. Old Woodruff puffed Woodbines almost non-stop, and a customer had to be nifty to manoeuvre his head out of the way of the long ash. Chaps frequently emerged with grey Woodbine ash on their waistcoats or decorating their craniums. If Woodruff spied it he crouched, puffed out his cheeks, and blew the ash to the far side of the room.

Mrs Wheeler's job was to get the towels out and put them to warm in the oven part of the Yorkshire range. Old editions of the *Colne Valley Guardian* were spread across the coconut matting on the kitchen floor. Bath night was a serious business, and woe betide anyone who splashed the precious water over the bath edge.

There was always a fire in the main room on Friday nights. A rare treat. Apart from then it was only lit on high days and holidays, such as Christmas. Those not having their bath would be in there listening to the battery-operated wireless set.

It was all hands on deck to dole hot water out of the set pot for the lucky first bather, who was always Margaret. She used the carbolic soap from an aluminium dish, then was rubbed dry in one of the towels draped round the wooden clothes horse. With her flannel nightie on, the slightly greyer water was topped up. Kettles were refilled and returned to the hob. Then it was Granville's turn, finally their mother.

Great consternation ensued if anyone knocked at the door at that point of the procedures. It was supposed to be locked and bolted on Friday nights, but perhaps somebody might have popped out to bring some washing in and forgotten. If old Joe Wood or any other determined neighbour barged in there was one hell of a splash as a towelled figure hurtled in utter confusion into the other room. "Come back again in half an hour," the visitor heard a voice calling.

125

Poor old dad Gilbert was always last in the tin bath, by which time the grey water was a pea souper shade. He never demurred. That was the way life worked for some.

But there was a very good reason for it, according to his wife's reckoning. On those Friday evenings when he'd been to have his hair cut up at Woodruff's, she was convinced there would be a number of stray loose hairs still attached to his person. Should he have first go in the bath, some of those may slide off his neck and float on top of the water. The next one in couldn't be expected to waste time catching dad's floating hairs, with the water getting colder by the minute.

Everyone cleansed at last, it was his job to return everything to the cellar, with the bath hung on the meat hook again until next Friday.

Amami night for some. One hell of a night for others.

The exertions of bath night over, there was Saturday to look forward to, scrounging empty jam jars and pop bottles to get a copper or two in exchange at the Co-op. Then there was rat's tail hunting. Those whose dads worked in the mill dyehouse had more opportunity for ratting.

Most times boys were recompensed at the Town Hall with 1d a tail. Sometimes Granville had another Saturday job, mending Joe Wood's wooden leg, a great cumbersome affair before modern materials came out. The wooden leg was attached to Joe's knee with rubber bands, which sometimes swivelled round and fell off, leaving poor old Joe stranded. Then he yelled down the yard for Granville to put them on again. "Granville, Granville lad, ah'll give yer a halfpenny if tha'll come over here and fix me up." If he hadn't a halfpenny to spare then he offered Granville a ride on his horse instead.

One Whit Saturday Granville had to bring back the wireless battery which had been taken for recharging on the Friday evening. Off he went, resplendent in his new grey flannel suit, white shirt and new red tie. Granville was in such a tearing hurry that some of the wireless battery acid spilled onto his new trousers. His rat's tail catcher chums were all spruced up, it being Whitsuntide, trying to look as though they'd never even heard of a rat's tail, let alone done business with one. And there was a bigger carry-on at home than when his new cap went on its adventure to Manchester.

CHAPTER
EIGHTEEN

The Lullaby of Broadway

We did not have to endure transistors and taped "music" while shopping in the 1930s. John, our shop assistant before the Second World War took him off to the Middle East, was a Bing Crosby fan and crooned all day long behind the counter. *Shuffle Off To Buffalo*, *White Christmas* (even in the midst of a heatwave) and *Deep in the Heart of Texas* serenaded customers as they pondered twixt Fox's ginger biscuits or Huntley and Palmer's mixed creams. The biscuits were loose, in big tins. Customers used to try one to see which they liked best. John stood, paper bag in hand, quite happy to wait until the decision was made, in a dream world of his own.

Then maybe there'd be a duet, John and Mother "titivating" the shop windows, as she termed it, with *On the Sunny Side of the Street*.

Customers who might have been wondering how they could manage till next pay day would quickly catch the mood, smiles lighting up their faces, hope swelling in their hearts, as they twirled round the shop floor partnered by Mother or John.

The impromptu dance over, a few groceries were put "on tick" till pay day, and a bag of broken biscuits pushed into the basket "for a bit of fun". No one left the shop feeling as miserable as when they went in.

Dad never mastered the quickstep and foxtrot. He wasn't really interested, though he was as mad about singing as the rest of them. Therefore, when *Everybody's Doing It* — dancing — was the craze during the 1930s, Mother went for private lessons a couple of afternoons a week and roped the willing shop assistant in for evening dance sessions in the front room above the shop.

After crooning "Ba-ba-ba-boo" throughout the day, and twitching from left to right across the shop floorboards, attending to customers, John was still keen to dance to the records after the shop had closed. He had an enviable knack of being able to balance on his heels, from side to side. I thought it marvellous!

He even found time to try and instruct me in the correct verbal hesitations of "Goodnight Vi — e — e — e — nna, you city of a million memories". I never could get it to his satisfaction, but it gave him the perfect excuse to keep warbling it himself. The air would be alive with whistling — people seem to have lost that art these days. I think it did a far better job than its modern counterpart — drugs and tranquillizers. There were no side-effects — except happiness.

That was the time when the world was agog about the romance of Mrs Simpson and the king. Mother read all about it in the papers, and took photographs of Mrs Simpson, and sometimes film star Kay Francis, to the hairdresser to see if she could copy the style on her. She had an obsession for having her photograph taken too, draped, or wearing her white fox fur, at a studio in town.

John was also adept at woodwork, and in his spare time made a gramophone cabinet for us to house our records. We proudly stood it alongside the new radiogram up in the front room. Frequently, mother couldn't contain herself until the shop had closed to begin dancing. She used to run upstairs and play a few dance records, inspiring whoever was down below in the shop to grab whoever was available. Travellers, customers, strangers, even a cat wasn't immune to being swept along in an impromptu foxtrot or quickstep between the crates of Tizer and ginger beer.

"You oughta take it up, Joe lad," Dad was urged, as Florrie the coalman's wife, or Mrs Wood the fish and chip shop man's wife, whirled him round the creaking floorboards. "They say t' fat uns make t' best gliders."

Best of all, I enjoyed the evening dance sessions, when I was safely tucked up in bed, next door to the "Palais de Danse". Always, the session began with the sparkling *Lullaby of Broadway*, probably in the mistaken assumption that it would send us children to sleep.

Then followed spirited renderings of *I Gotta Rainbow Around My Shoulder*, with accompanying heavy-footed thuds round the room. The rainbow "fitting like a glove" led onto smoochy melodies such as

Ramona, I'll Meet You by the Waterfall and *Tina, When the Leaves are a' Falling, Won't You Come Back to Me?*

Halfway through the evening, when the dancers needed "a breather," a smoke and a bit of refreshment, they listened to monologues and drank Dandelion and Burdock or Tizer.

One of our prized records was Stanley Holloway reciting *The Lion and Albert*, and another was *Sam, Sam, Pick up tha' Musket*. Then there was that one about Henry the Eighth and his wives, one of whom "walked the draughty corridor, for miles and miles she walked, with her head tucked underneath her arm, at the midnight hour".

I breathed a sigh of relief when that one was over and they began thudding round again, interrupted spasmodically by sudden yells of anguish if John's heavy boots came down on Mother's silver dancing shoes, or if Prince, the family collie, happened to have a paw in the way.

When I listened to one record, *Don't Hang My Harry*, I relived the moments leading up to 8a.m. on a hanging morning, imagining how it would be, alive and well one minute, knowing that the next you would be hung from the neck in prison, executed, probably, by Albert Pierrepoint. I made up my mind there and then that I would never put myself in a position where I needed to be hanged! The record continued, "we never could bear to part, and remember that when you are breaking his neck, you are breaking his poor mother's heart". I wonder if anyone still has a copy of that?

After that gruesome song Mother usually crept into the bedroom to see if I was asleep, telling me it was "high time I was" if I wasn't. Then it was off back into the front room above the shop to put on another dance tune.

There was no need for alcohol. The music was intoxication enough. Who could fail to respond to the invitation:

> Come along and listen to,
>   The lullaby of Broadway,
> The hip hooray and ballyhoo
> ,   The rumble of the taxi.
> Goodnight, Baby, sleep tight, Baby,
>   Milkman's on his way.

Philip and I knew the evening's dancing was drawing to a close when a final record was put on, and John and mother joined in singing:

> Oh! Give me a home, where the buffalo roam,
>   Where the deer and the antelope play.
> Where seldom is heard a discouraging word,
>   And the skies are not cloudy all day.

So well did John copy the singing of a famous singing cowboy of the 1930s that when at last the front room door opened for him to leave, I fully expected to hear a white horse snorting its way downstairs with him.

Dad never bothered to learn how to dance. He maintained with a grin that Mother led him a big enough dance as it was.

CHAPTER
NINETEEN

Kenneth

In the 1920s Joseph Greenwood ran a thriving ladies' and gent's tailoring and drapery business at 9 Diamond Street, Moldgreen. Gentlemen looking for a tailor to make up a suit length were often recommended there. As Joseph was a credit draper, customers were not obliged to pay at once. They were allowed twenty weeks.

The stone terrace house had three bedrooms, one which was used as his workroom. Two days weekly Joseph drove his motorbike and sidecar round the Scissett and Clayton West areas, selling drapery. The goods could be purchased "on appro", meaning on approval.

His son, Kenneth, born in May 1929, was definitely approved of. He was Joseph and Edith's only child, although Betty, one of their nieces, was brought up in their home too.

Joseph used best-quality cloth, and was nonplussed when, in the early 1930s, a gentleman client from Edgerton, where all the toffs lived, asked for a suit to be made, but queried the modest price. *He* must have the very best cloth. When told that *was* the best, he still maintained that top quality must surely cost more. Hadn't Joseph any better pattern books? In a quandary, Joseph asked the wholesaler Joseph Booth, on Byram Street, what he should do. "Show him the same books, but double the price", he recommended. Joseph did, and it worked like a charm. "That's more like it, my man," smiled the client.

Relations lived round about, a cluster of security for little Kenneth. His mother's sister, Caroline Tempest Jessop, lived next door, and Joseph's two unmarried sisters at No. 10. Joseph and Edith stayed with Grandad Thomas Kaye Whittell, a French polisher, as he was widowed just before their wedding.

For some years Joseph was ill. His doctor thought he might be healthier if he was outside more, with more exercise. But it was to no avail, and on 27 April 1933, aged only 35, Joseph passed away. An obituary related how the tailor never failed to be optimistic and cheerful, despite ill health, and had a welcoming smile for all.

The funeral tea, in the Co-op Café, Huddersfield, was a day to remember in more ways than one. Kenneth, who hadn't been to the burial, had no idea why he was being taken to the Co-op Café for tea. Leaning back against the door of the taxi, it burst open, and the four-year-old fell out. It was his début on the stage of life. The small boy ran in the tram lines on John William Street after the retreating taxi. His absence was noticed, and the mourners continued on their way when he was retrieved.

It was a sad year for the family. In the autumn, Betty, only ten years old, died from dropsy.

Edith realised there were still some drapery accounts which had to be collected, and that she would have to find some means of earning money to supplement the 10s widow's pension and the 5s allowed for Kenneth.

"Why don't *you* bring us the drapery round, Mrs Greenwood?" customers asked, probably thinking that looking at intimate garments would be easier with one of their own kind. Well, there was nothing to stop her. Grandad Whittell was there, and Kenneth's aunties and cousins on either side of them.

The arrangement suited Kenneth. Grandad didn't hold with the new-fangled wireless, as it stopped a fellow reading his newspaper. So there wasn't one in No. 9. But Kenneth could have his tea with one of his aunties if his mother wasn't back from her drapery rounds. He could listen to *Children's Hour* on their wireless at the same time. Tales of Toytown, Romany and Raq his dog, Auntie Muriel, Auntie Doris and Uncle Mac were auntie and uncle to all the children who tuned in to the wireless programme every weekday.

After Edith decided to continue the drapery business, going on the early morning bus to Scissett carrying two suitcases, come hail, rain, sunshine or show, teatime at the house became "a movable feast". Anything could happen. People were forever popping in to "have a look at what you've got new, Edith". The room was a riot of brown paper, balls of string and drapery. Grandad wanted attention, and let it be known

136

with an exasperated, "Edith, aren't we going to have us tea? Let's get one job done at once!"

The drapery round took a fixed route, with Edith leaving at 8.30a.m. with stockings, knickers, vests and dresses — Macclesfield silk ones in stripes were highly fashionable, and perfect for seaside holidays. Clients became friends, and Edith was sure to be invited in for a meal with one or other of them. It was a big event in a customer's life if she ventured into the Huddersfield warehouse to try a dress on when Edith had given them a note. This meant she didn't have to carry big stocks with her.

Kenneth loved all the hustle and bustle, and being surrounded with people. He didn't have any set amount for spending money, but earned coppers doing errands for his mother and aunties. To Gawkrodgers and Hardy's shops, the Co-op and the butchers.

One day in 1938 his mother asked him to go to the butcher's for some liver. When he returned she thought he had too much change. "Which butcher did you get it from, Kenneth?" she wanted to know, nearly having a fit when he said, "Argenta". "It'll be frozen — we're not having that kind of stuff here," Edith remonstrated, and cooked it for the cat. Kenneth was sent to the usual shop for *proper* liver. When the war came they were glad of any kind.

Kenneth loved to buy a yard of toffee for ½d, or a whirl of liquorice with a pink sweet in the centre. Lucky bags were ½d, and he also favoured sherbet dabs. Gobstoppers were a bit worrying, as life could be snuffed out in a second if one stuck in the throat. It was thought "below par" to buy chewing gum. Edith considered it looked "common stuff", but really was concerned that it might stick in Kenneth's windpipe and choke him. Dinky toys and Meccano parts were cheap enough to buy when he had earned a few coppers by going errands.

As befitted the son of a tailor, Kenneth was always smartly dressed. His dad formerly made his outfits, but then his mother took him to The Boys' Shop on New Street in Huddersfield.

One Whitsuntide he was looking forward to wearing his new suit and shirt, now that he was old enough to stop wearing the blouses and jerseys with matching knitted ties that small boys habitually wore during the 1930s. He could always tell who were the poor boys in his class at school, as they didn't have matching ties with their jerseys.

Anyhow, Whit Sunday dawned bright and sunny, but Kenneth had an additional colour scheme — a bright red rash. It turned out to be German measles. How disappointed he was that the new suit hanging in the wardrobe could not be worn that day. How aggravating that illness didn't strike on a school day, but on a bank holiday.

Another memorable Whitsuntide for Kenneth was when the tar on the road melted, it was so hot. Somehow or other he wandered into the road instead of keeping on the pavement. First it got onto his new shoes, then, in his attempt to rub it off, marks appeared on his new shirt and knee-length socks.

138

Kenneth became a choirboy at Moldgreen Congregational Sunday school, occasionally singing a solo, such as *Jerusalem* or *The Holy City*. Roger Braithwaite was the parson. He used to make up a story to tell the children every Sunday morning about a girl called Tomboy, who was always in some kind of a predicament when it was time for the children to go home. What better ploy of making sure scholars went back the following Sunday to find out what happened to Tomboy next!

Grandad sent his collars to "Collars Ltd, Dry Cleaners". They were returned in a cardboard box, which he used as a container for his few necessities when going on holiday. His bowler hat was a necessity, but that remained on his head. All he took with him was a towel, razor, flannel, and two striped "fronts" for his one shirt, which he also slept in. (He had plenty of shirts, but only wore one for a week or so at a time.) There was no need for underpants then, as shirts had long flaps at the back which were pulled under and up to cover the bits that had to be covered. Tom didn't wear vests.

He kept his old bowler hat, with a muffler, hanging over the lavatory key, which dangled on a bit of string by the door. If the hat had been removed, his anxious cry went up: "Edith, have yer seen owt o' me closet cap?"

One of Tom's pleasures in old age was joining a few pals down in the snug at the Somerset Arms to have a drink and "tell the tale". They once drew a horse in the Irish Sweep, ten of them sharing a few pounds, but it was a thrill nevertheless, and one which probably helped with expenses when Grandad went with Kenneth and the boy's Uncle Cyril to Blackpool in 1937.

The family had cousins who kept a boarding house in Scarborough, so they alternated between Northern seaside resorts for their annual summer holiday. The resort was determined by where the dancing competitions were held. Cousin Margaret Jessop attended dancing lessons at a class in Somerset Road, Moldgreen, and it was a heady event when they all went to cheer her on in a contest. If it was staged in Blackpool, Edith and her family stayed at Mrs Sunley's boarding house — "Three minutes from the sea." Kenneth used to grumble, "Only if you're an Olympic athlete."

While his cousins pirouetted in pretty dresses, Kenneth spent a lot of time wearing his woollen swimming costume in those glorious 1930s summers, unless they were going for a walk on the Sunday, or to church, when he wore his smart best suit, shirt, tie and knee-length socks. Even when it was hot. Grandad wore a dark suit, waistcoat, Cherry Blossom polished black shoes and the inevitable bowler hat. Uncle Cyril preferred a trilby.

When Kenneth was only young and restless in bed, unable to sleep, his mother continued with her ironing or whatever housework she was doing downstairs and left the door open so he could hear her singing, which made the work pass more enjoyably for her as well, there being no wireless in the house.

The usual lullaby was about a little coloured boy. Edith's version was this:

When Mammy on her lap, took the weeping little
 chap
And sang in her kind old way, "Now stay this side
 of the high board fence
.Don't mind what them white childes do,
Just go out and play, just as much as you please,
But stay in your own backyard."

If that didn't do the trick, other songs followed: *Keep the Home Fires Burning, The Sunshine of Your Smile.* Songs that have stood the test of time, and will go on doing so.

Christmas heralded even more hustle, bustle and good-natured banter down Diamond Street. All the relations surrounded the turkey, each year declaring the present one to be the biggest ever seen. The usual weight was 24lb. Mrs Armitage, Auntie Maud's mother, had a butcher's shop, and considered herself a bit of an expert at making sausages. Christmas was certainly a family occasion. Auntie Maud slept with Edith, Uncle Cyril somewhere else — maybe in the same bedroom as Grandad and Kenneth. On Christmas Eve Grandad brought home a few old cronies from the Liberal Club to help the festivities along. Herbert Shore brought his violin, and Kenneth sang *Bless This House*, secretly hoping his pillowcase, hanging from the mantelpiece, would be amply blessed. How they accommodated so many bodies — neighbours were irresistibly drawn to the good-humoured throng — was a miracle. But then, miracles do happen at Christmas time don't they?

Santa never failed Kenneth. A bicycle, a chocolate Father Christmas and other novelties, tins of Mackintosh's toffee with pictures of an Aberdeen terrier or fluffy kitten on them, *Boy's Own Annual*, Billy Bunter and Greyfriars adventures to read in another annual, games, selection boxes, and smokers' outfits, made of sweets, of course. The problem was, which to start on first. In 1940 Santa even left him a typewriter as well as all the other stuff!

At five o'clock on a Christmas morning, though the family had barely been in bed above three or four hours, up they rose to go down to the kitchen for the ritual of basting the turkey. "The biggest one we've ever seen," was murmured over and over again as the fat dribbled over the splendid chest. After cups of tea, the turkey basters trooped back to bed. But in no time at all it was all hands on deck again. Edith's two sisters-in-law had the job of boiling the potatoes and vegetables in their house, and Auntie Carrie was responsible for the Yorkshire puddings, which were eaten as the first course, with luscious onion gravy. Sage and onion stuffing, apple sauce, cranberry, bread sauce and similar delicacies were Edith's domain. Christmas puddings wrapped in canvas were boiled in the cleaned-out set pot. Then there was the rum sauce to be made. It was hard work, but ever so enjoyable.

The men ate first as they were keen to get off to the rugby match between Huddersfield and Halifax at Fartown in the afternoon. The air filled with the delicious aroma of fat Havana cigars as fans walked to the ground, and a brass band played carols before and in the interval at the match.

If Christmas Day fell on a Sunday, they all went to church. When Grandad and Cyril and whoever else was with them returned elated or deflated as the case may be, another "spread" awaited them. Pork pies, pickled onions, cold turkey and accompaniments, mince pies and cheese, Christmas cake, and "tots" of port and lemon. A jolly evening followed with piano playing, carols and lots of gaiety. The following week the happy family reconvened to see in another New Year.

CHAPTER
TWENTY

Saturday — the Best Day of the Week

If a vote had to be taken about the best day of the week, most children would not hesitate to say Saturday. I enjoyed cleaning out the hen hut in the henyard, hanging clean white net curtains at the window, and pinning a drawing or two I'd painted on the walls. Sunday was too near Monday, but Saturday spread out in front of me with complete freedom. Time to spend the weekend ½d or 1d, which more or less had to be on bubble gum if a series of pictures was given away free with it. I was lucky, living at a shop. I could look at the pictures first, and make sure I didn't get one of a film star that I already had.

Children hung round outside the shop door waiting for workmen who had come in to buy cigarettes. As they came out the children pounced.

"Have you any cig cards, Mister? Can I have 'em, please?" The request sometimes resulted in an "Aye, here you are, lad" and a whoop of delight if the card turned out to be of a cricketer or footballer missing from a nearly completed set.

144

Themes were in sets of fifty usually. Much swapping went on between schoolboys: "I'll give you two Len Hutton for one of Don Bradman", or whoever it was they needed.

Will's cigarettes included famous names such as Yorkshire's Herbert Sutcliffe and E. Oldroyd. Then there was a series of gardening hints and another called "Do You Know?" which was a far more acceptable method of teaching to the ordinary boy than sitting in a classroom learning by rote. There was the thrill of the chase, and competing to reach a full set first.

Older boys joined the YMCA and played football for the team on Saturday afternoons, some strutting there with a Charlie Chaplin gait, feet turned out and twirling a stick in their hands.

Player's cigarettes ran a series of fifty motor cars, and for a 1d, collectors could buy an album specially prepared to hold the complete series. De Reszke — "The Aristocrat of Cigarettes" — ran a series of real photographs, twenty-seven in each, mainly featuring animals in cute poses or film stars. "That Kruschen Feeling" showed a dog leaping high over a fence, indicating that's what people taking Kruschen Salts would feel like doing. Sometimes smokers chucked the card nonchalantly in the gutter. What a scramble ensued among eagle-eyed collectors!

Children of large families often didn't have any money to spend on Saturday sweets. They had to do *something* to earn it. One Saturday morning local lad Sam asked his pals what they dared him to do "for a tanner". It was a hot sunny afternoon, and the milkman's horse and cart had been round. "Dare yer to eat some of that, Sam," his pals jeered and laughed. Sam was desperate. He picked a piece up, grinned, and sauntered down the middle of the road showing off. He earned his 6*d*. His bubble gum would taste all the sweeter after his first course!

Saturday matinées were for devotees of cowboys and Indians. Ken Maynard, Tom Mix and his horse Tony, Gene Autry, the Singing Cowboy. Great favourites were Laurel and Hardy, the cartoons of Mickey Mouse, Pluto and entourage, and Popeye the Sailor Man. A few of the boys sang lewd lyrics to the latter, to the dismay of the usherette who swivelled her torch along the rows in an effort to cool their ardour. Charlie Chaplin had a great following, as did Peter Lorre, he with the odd-looking, rolling eyes.

Snow White and the Seven Dwarfs was showing at the Regent in 1938. After a few friends had been to our house for tea, mother took all of us to see the new full-length film instead of playing games as we usually did. We were charmed by the colour, and sang the songs *Whistle While You Work; Heigh ho, Heigh ho, It's Off to Work We Go* and *Some Day My Prince Will Come* as we walked back home.

Queuing outside cinemas was the *only* way to spend a Saturday night, unless you were older and went dancing, scanning the evening *Examiner* to decide which film sounded the best. There were so many to choose from. The bus to the terminus if the cinema was in town, then "fish and a penn'orth", eating from the bag with fingers. Piping hot. Delicious! Better than a meal in the Waldorf!

Grown-ups became marvellous mimics after seeing a Charlie Chan film, imitating the character played by Warner Oland as we had tea and biscuits at home, or frightening each other pretending to be Boris Karloff as the Monster.

Reading in bed was a satisfactory ending to a Saturday, with the glorious knowledge that tomorrow was Sunday, and there was no need to put the alarm clock on. And if you went to Sunday school, it didn't begin until ages after weekday school did.

Saturday. Freedom. Long walks in country lanes and woods. Books. Non-stop pleasure. Oh, that Saturday was every day of the week.

When I was eleven, and feeling quite grown-up, I wanted to give Dad something different for his birthday on 2 April. What better for springtime than a new trilby? A BIG PRESENT. Not just a tie or socks.

I wanted to do the transaction entirely by myself. Into town I went, heart throbbing with pride at the big surprise I intended, smartly dressed in my dusky pink, Heatonex flecked tweed coat with stitched, plum-coloured velvet collar and buttons, and matching close-fitting hat with turned-back velvet brim. Half boldly, half timidly, I pushed open the door of Dunns, Gentleman's Outfitter, on New Street, a beautifully appointed establishment, with mahogany fittings, brass handles on drawers, and an air of quiet dignity. A gentleman in a black suit deferentially approached.

147

"Good morning, young miss. Can I help you?" I described what I wanted, and regarded the gentleman's head, not being quite sure of the size. I had looked inside the brim of an old trilby belonging to dad, but the size number had faded. 6¾ was decided upon as the most likely size, and I selected a dark green one with a little red and green feather jauntily jutting out at the side of the hat band. It might transform dad into looking like Robin Hood (or Errol Flynn). I handed over 7s 11d, by which time the gentleman's outfitter and I were on the very best of terms, with an assurance that if the hat didn't fit, Dad would have no need to wear it. It could be exchanged. Then the door was held open for me, and, with a slight inclination of the head and a friendly, courteous smile, he thanked me for my custom, and did hope the gentleman would like the trilby and have a very happy birthday.

I'd had my reservations about making such an important transaction by myself, but came out glowing with pleasure, clutching the brown bag with "Dunns, Gentleman's Outfitter" across the side. What a civilized way to go shopping! A perfect Saturday morning. Daring to do something I'd never attempted before had been far more exhilarating than sticking in the same old groove at home, and I'd made a new friend into the bargain. How I loved smart, civilized gentlemen like the ones who attended customers in Dunns.

The only worry then was what if Dad wore it to the Saturday night cinema, and left the new trilby under the seat?

Sometimes I practised the piano on Saturday afternoons, in the front room over the shop. First the set homework pieces, then looking through the sheet music in the music stool: *Robin's Return, Kitten on the Keys, I'm Forever Blowing Bubbles*, waltzes and Victor Sylvester's dance tunes, costing 6d each from Wood's music shop or Woolworths, the finale being what all children rattled off best — played fast:

> O can you wash my father's shirt,
> O can you wash it clean?
> O can you wash my father's shirt
> And send it to the Queen?

I imagined any customers downstairs in the shop staring wide-eyed in amazement at each other. What a child prodigy upstairs! Especially when I finished with a flourish of fingernails zooming the length of the keys then back again.

If a knock came at the back door, followed by "Are you coming out to play, kid?" from some friend or other, any piano interlude came to a swift close.

I might go into the garden to see how my patch of vegetables was progressing. Seeds and implements were kept in the disused stone privy up in the top corner, with a dropping-to-pieces chair for a rest after my exertions, and for listening in to customers to-ing and fro-ing unaware of my presence behind the high wall.

I wondered what our customers looked like in bed. If roofs could be miraculously lifted off for a few fleeting moments, with me airborne on a magic carpet

149

overhead, then I could look down and see them all, heads on pillows, asleep. It annoyed me intensely that some aspects of life, such as seeing what our customers looked like lying down instead of lounging over counters, fully dressed, were as impossible to know as flying to the moon.

Anyhow, Saturday was too full of possibilities to moan about what may not be, so how about trying to bake a chocolate cake, or brandy snap? Licking the bowl out was the best bit. Or how about walking on walls, or avoiding cracks in pavements? Step on a crack and one's whole life could be jeopardized. Some preferred to cartwheel or handstand against walls, dresses tucked into navy knickers, to while away the freedom of Saturday. Or playing ball games. What permutations — throwing a ball against a wall, spinning wildly round before catching it, clapping, whizzing it beneath a leg, one, two, three a lara, four, five six — chanting on and on the whole day long.

I hated somersaults, cartwheels and all that carry on. I far preferred music. We had a wonderland of records to play on our radiogram. Richard Tauber, Peter Dawson, Heddle Nash, Webster Booth and Anne Zeigler, the Huddersfield Choral Society, Gilbert and Sullivan, and loads more. What glorious words that "Street Singer" of the 1930s, Arthur Tracy, sang! Songs with divine titles like *South Sea Island Magic*. I played one part over and over again, when the Street Singer spoke these words:

For life is a game,
And we all play our part,
Rich man, beggar, the King.
We all have our troubles,
Dug deep in our hearts
But smile we must, and laugh, and sing.
We're here just one day, you and I
,And even the sweetest of flowers are destined to
    die,
So help one another, it's the least to attempt,
For sooner or later, no one is exempt,
Broken-hearted clown, though inside we know
    you'll cry,
The show is ending, the curtain is down, broken
    hearted clown.

Another song was called *Stay Awhile:*

So let our hearts be gay awhile,
When hearts are young don't go away, please stay
    awhile.

We had some beggars, or as near to beggars as
can be, among our customers, and how glad I was
that Dad and Mother gave many a bag of broken
biscuits and other free hand-outs to *our* "broken
hearted clowns".
A new record had been released about Mickey
Mouse which I also loved to play. It went something
like this:

151

All the world is so excited,
And the kids are all delighted,
For the stork has brought a son and daughter
To Mr and Mrs Mickey Mouse.

I bet they arrived on a Saturday.

CHAPTER
TWENTY-ONE

Scarlet Fever Isolation Hospital

Geoff Hill was born in 1935 at Northgate, Aldmondbury, in a row of cottages owned by George and Elsie Mellor. Though no blood relations, Geoff and his sister Joan and younger brother Raymond called them Uncle and Auntie, in the friendly manner adopted by neighbours in the 1920s and 1930s. The Mellors gave the family cabbages, and were concerned about their welfare.

Geoff was upset when the Mellors removed to Thurstonland. He soon went to visit them, and Auntie gave him a jam jar from the farm full of frogspawn. Geoff kept it on the kitchen windowsill at home, and it all turned into tadpoles, but only two or three into frogs.

Geoff, when small, enjoyed visiting a neighbour who gave him slices of bread and butter "like thick doorsteps", liberally doused with tomato ketchup. She was known to all and sundry — but not to Geoff — as Mucky Alice. Pigeons and hens roamed all over the place.

When Mr Hill joined up in the war, the family left Aldmondbury to live with their Grandma at 49 Riddings Rise, Sheepridge. None of them considered themselves to be poor, despite having to go to the Cinderella Society in Byram Arcade, Huddersfield, for "new" shoes. Before Geoff started school his mother used to take him to Castlegate for his Grandma to take care of him. Until his mother found a job helping at Whittaker's fish and chip shop there was only his dad's army pay to keep the family.

The children walked to Woodhouse School for their dinners. Geoff recalls Dan Appleyard delivering milk by horse and cart round Riddings, playing hide and seek behind privet hedges, and when the war began a pig bin for household scraps was placed opposite their house. With the new council estate there were too many children all to be accommodated at Deighton School, so a couple of upstairs rooms at the Maypole pub, Brackenhall, became a temporary school for some.

Geoff delivered newspapers before school when aged nine, and gave his earnings to his mother. On a Saturday he plaintively asked, "Can I go to the Rialto? Peter Briggs is going." "They don't call you Peter Briggs!" came back the sharp reply.

Sixpenny back seats at the cinema had been restored in green velvet. Geoff didn't aspire to one of those. But there were 3d and 4d ones as well. Serials were always shown on a Saturday afternoon, and a child would move heaven and earth to go the following week to see what happened next. Perhaps the hero had been left

154

dangling over a cliff — could he hang on and not fall the rest of the way before next Saturday afternoon?

When the children emerged from the dark cinema they reenacted the scenes they had witnessed on the screen, slapping their thighs and galloping on their fiery steeds if it had been a cowboy movie or pointing "guns" at unsuspecting passers-by and shouting "Bang! Bang! Bang! You're dead!"

If an air raid started a notice was flashed onto the screen: "There is an air raid in progress." Those who were more concerned with reality left, while those more concerned about having paid to see the picture stayed.

When Geoff and his pals ran home the feeling was more of excitement than fear. It was quite picturesque to see the searchlights raking the skies during an air raid in 1941, and later to find bits of shrapnel that had bounced off anti-aircraft guns. Shrapnel bits during the 1940s were schoolboy treasures.

In 1940 Geoff was a keen marbles player. They were his real treasures. He had a dried milk tin full of them, including some of the cheapest type, clay ones, "which didn't last two minutes". It was a regular sight to see boys crouched on pavements absorbed in the game. When Geoff had a ½d or a 1d he bought more marbles at a little shop near the Rialto.

One day Geoff was ill, very ill, and had a bright red rash. He was rushed off to Mill Hill Isolation Hospital at Dalton and remained there for thirteen weeks in a mixed ward, missing his beloved marbles like mad. Visitors weren't allowed to be in direct contact with the children — a window was always between them.

However, one day his dad, on leave from the army, decided to go and see his son, who by that time had reached the playing-out-in-the-grounds stage. So his dad thought nothing about walking in and joining the convalescent children on the lawns. Matron "went scatty" when she spied him! And poor Geoff was convinced, as he was then better, that he'd been put in a Home where he would have to stay until he grew up. What a prospect!

When the day of release arrived, Geoff's first thought was of his imminent reunion with the marbles waiting in the dried milk tin. But it wasn't to be. His homecoming was completely blighted when his Grandma informed him, "I threw those filthy things away. That's where you picked up scarlet fever, playing with marbles near the drains." That was an even worse moment than looking in his locker every morning and finding his clothes still there. If they had gone, it meant they had been taken to be fumigated, and going home was imminent.

But for that longed-for moment to arrive, and then the very treasures he had dreamt about for so long to have been wantonly thrown away — all those wasted halfpennies — now he would have to start all over again. Can any pangs of loss match those of a boy who has lost his beloved marbles? Geoff didn't think so. To make matters worse, his four-year-old cousin had died as well, from TB he thought, or it might have been diphtheria.

Still, he was home. There were Saturdays at the "flicks" to look forward to again, and that steep banking behind Beaumont's Farm at the back of the school. He wondered if it was still as steep as when he went into the hospital. How thrilling it was to a small boy, standing on the summit and gazing down the steep slope, wondering, "Dare I set off at a run?", knowing from experience the heady sensation of running and gaining such momentum and speed that he couldn't stop until the flat field was reached. It was more thrilling even than going on the Big Dipper at Blackpool, and all that excitement cost absolutely nothing, not even the price of a marble. Rolling down the banking, over and over again, was wizard too. And if he could get hold of an empty barrel, then the excitement knew no bounds. He might even try out his old cart with the pram wheels and lengths of string for steering with. An optimistic outlook was the answer, Geoff realised. Think of something else to do when you lose something.

Like when his dad went off to be a soldier, his mother took them all to be photographed at Geoffrey's on New Street, to send one to his dad. He may not be able to see and talk to his family face to face, but he did have photograph to remind him of them.

Life is made up of compensations, even though now Geoff was back at home tea merely consisted of a slice of bread with lard spread on and sprinkled with salt, when he ran in from playing in the garden.

But what a day when the war was declared to be over! His mother went down to Taylor's shop when it was first known celebrations would soon be in order, and street parties were being organized. "Could Joe bake a big, big VE Day cake, decorated in red, white and blue?" Of course he could, and did. Everybody on the estate contributed food of some description, and Mrs Hill made an outsize, wobbly pink blancmange.

Later that year Geoff went to the Regent cinema, which was further to walk to than the Rialto. The usherette warned the youngsters, "Close your eyes when the scenes of Belsen are shown." But shutting one's eyes to horrible conditions doesn't make the atrocities disappear. Perhaps it's beneficial to show these wrongs, as it shows what effect bullying can have.

CHAPTER
TWENTY-TWO

Childhood on Apple Tree Farm

Children born into a family owning their own business were far better off materially than those depending on one wage and the whims of an employer. Many youngsters in the 1920s, 1930s and 1940s never even had their photograph taken unless it was on a school group — and then many parents couldn't afford to buy a copy.

How different it was for Lenora Mellor, born in 1936, and Tony, in 1940. Their parents owned Apple Tree Farm, Stocksmoor. Mrs Mellor took her children to Greave's studio in Huddersfield every year to capture their childhood forever. Someone in the family must have had a camera, maybe one of those Box Brownies, as their father, Charles Roger Mellor, was snapped in Cross Road Field with one of the dogs, Floss, resting against a stile. They even managed to get films in wartime. So, compared to many youngsters, the family were "living in clover".

Of course, a good living doesn't arrive by idleness. Life on a farm may appear idyllic, but it is hard work with long hours. However, a farmer and his family did not have the nagging daily worry about unemployment as did so many during "The Hungry Thirties". Lenora and Tony even had a playroom in the vast, old farmhouse, big enough for them to have a full scale table tennis set in it. They had a bedroom each, plenty of wholesome food, barns in which to play, fields and woods around them, and clothes were certainly no problem.

But the children were expected to help with the chores. On Sunday mornings and during the holidays Lenora often went delivering milk, driving a horse and cart, either with Bob, a Welsh cob, or Bonnie, the Suffolk Punch. Bob could be a bit temperamental. One Sunday he bolted, with Lenora hanging onto the reins. She was quite frightened, but one of the farm workers, Harry Harrison, in true *Boy's Own* manner, sprinted across a field and jumped in front of runaway Bob, bringing him to a halt. Unaccustomed noises, gunfire and other sudden disturbances can soon upset an animal.

Betty Jackson was another employee, helping round the farm with whatever needed doing. Milk was taken out in big churns, then ladled into jugs. Customers often gave the horse a bit of bread or carrot to help it on its way. Edna Jenkinson, who lived in Norton Terrace, usually had a mug full of delicious home-made soup ready for the milkman or girl on winter days. Vegetable or chicken, how welcome it was! Mr Mellor bought an ounce of Bruno tobacco daily from Walter Charlesworth's shop on Cross Lane. Bonnie and Bob were not forgotten. They had a packet of Smith's potato crisps, and the children shared one of those flat packets of Wrigley's chewing gum.

Tony collected cigarette cards, exchanging those he might get two of with his pals, David Jenkinson, David Ownsworth and Michael Wood. The boys loved helping on the farm. When you're young, a farm is one big playground, and certainly not classed as work!

Leonora and Tony didn't have set amounts of spending money. Everything they needed was right there. But while life on the farm was interesting, varied and often fun, danger lurked if you weren't careful. Before the Mellors took over, a Mr and Mrs Taylor lived at Apple Tree Farm. Mr Taylor was in a field with one of his horses and a cart when the harness broke, the horse stumbled, the cart went over him, and Mr Taylor's back was broken.

At threshing time when Tony was a boy he often created havoc. Frequently his Uncle George, from Woodend Farm, resorted to putting his small nephew in a hessian sack, tying him up and hanging it on a hook to be out of danger's way. Tony fooled about in the stackyard, clambering onto a side building, and racing backwards and forwards in bursts of youthful energy. A friend of Lenora, Molly Pontefract, once went there to play. Tony teased her, then, after a heated exchange, from his advantageous position, he hurled a stone at his adversary. It caught Bob, the horse, instead, making the animal leap sky high.

Although Lenora adored all animals, Tony was instrumental in making her terrified of hens. He used to gather them up in his arms then make a rush at Lenora, "fluttering" them at his sister. It was a long time before she even dare touch a baby chicken.

When Lenora had her birthday party, on 1st November, she made sure it was an all-girl affair, Tony being there on sufferance! Though like most brothers and sisters, sibling rivalry was merely an added excitement to the very real affection that existed between them. (Lenora visits Tony every week from her home in Whitby, now that they are grown up, and the teasing has stopped.) Rows and fights — when they don't get completely out of hand — are half the fun of growing up.

On the farm was a machine with teeth which was used for breaking up slabs of cattle food. Exactly at the moment one of the farm workers turned the handle, Tony decided to stick his fingers in it. What a horrible mess it made of his hand, and the scars are still evident.

The children's maternal grandparents, Mr and Mrs Ernest Carter, lived at Springwood, Huddersfield. Sometimes they visited them at Christmas, but more often they ran across to Yew Tree Farm, where their other Grandma and Grandad lived. That Grandma used to put warm milk in a basin and leave it overnight, using the cream on top for Tony's porridge.

Rover, an Alsatian, and Rex, a sheepdog, were Lenora and Tony's perpetual chums. Always there ready for a game, even when human playmates arrived late because of drifting snow or dark nights. In 1947 there were snowdrifts up to twelve and thirteen feet high in the surrounding fields, and seven or eight feet round the farmhouse. Charles harnessed one of the horses to a big sledge in an effort to take milk crates to Stocksmoor Station, and Tony and Lenora were unable to make a way through to school because of the atrocious weather. Eventually, a thaw set in, and springtime, shuttlecocks, battledores, whips and tops returned to isolated Apple Tree Farm. Building snowmen and sledging in the snows of 1947 gradually became only a memory.

The summer of 1947 was as gloriously perfect as the winter had resembled a Victorian Christmas card. Every June, Dickinson's rolled up to Apple Tree Farm, to the great delight of children, pulling the threshing machine by steam engine. The fields were full of hay "stooks" in the shape of wigwams. Children played cowboys and Indians, hide and seek, running and plopping down onto them. Rats, unearthed by the unaccustomed activity, proliferated in fields and barns. But eager dogs took care of those — though one can't help but feel sorry for any living creature trying to make a living for itself.

That summer of '47 steam trains spewing out red-hot cinders set fire to the railway banking at Stocksmoor. Trout in nearby streams were found suffocated, floating on top. But Tony thrived, spending most of that wonderful summer holiday in his swimming costume, which must have cut down on washing for his mother. Bluebells filled the woods and life was very heaven.

The threshers were given a huge breakfast at Apple Tree Farm before they started work in the fields.

Bacon, eggs, the lot. At midday there was a cooked dinner, and a ham salad tea, with many cups of tea and coffee in between and in the evening. Threshing lasted a couple of days.

Joking, Mr Dickinson wondered if a pig had been killed for him to take home? In the war farmers were fined if they were found to have been killing pigs solely for their own use, and a dead pig could be confiscated. However, there was a lot of "black marketeering" going on, and men from the ministry couldn't have their snouts in every nook and cranny.

Mr Mellor didn't take time off from farm duties to have a holiday, but Mrs Mellor and the children occasionally enjoyed a week at Blackpool.

As the nights began to "draw in", when autumn came round again, the radiogram in the farm began to be used more often, and Lenora and Tony's thoughts raced ahead to Christmas. There was ample room for Father Christmas, and his reindeer too, to slither down the enormous Yorkshire range fireplace in the massive-beamed farm kitchen, so Christmas held no worries on that score when they pencilled letters to their hero and sent them flying up the big open chimney.

Not merely pillowcases, but full-length bolster cases were hung up on Christmas Eve, with no anxieties about them not being full to overflowing next morning. Still, the children *had* earned the rewards showered on them, what with delivering milk at weekends and in the school holidays, and assisting with the thousand and one other tasks around the farm.

What an Aladdin's cave there was to plunder on the early morning of 25th December — bikes, prams, a doll's cot and pram, doll's house, doll's furniture, blackboard and easel, lots of board games, magician sets, a Hornby train set, and books galore, such as *Chatterbox, Boys' Own Annual* and *Girls' Own Annual*.

Going to church on Sunday evenings began each new week, praising God from whom all blessings flow. And when your childhood is lived on a farm in an idyllic, rural setting, blessings are bountiful indeed.

TWENTY-THREE

The Ice-Cream Manufacturer's Daughter

Having a dad who made ice-cream would, you'd think, be every child's dream come true. But Pauline Frith, a war baby, born 16 December 1940, never had a "sweet tooth", which was just as well, coming into a world of rationing and shortages. Stanley, her dad, owned an ice-cream business at Green Cross, Moldgreen. He won competitions all over before the war, including at Olympia. Pauline, the eldest of three girls, spent many hours in a large pram at 253 Wakefield Road.

When sugar rationing came into force Stanley Frith rose to the challenge by inventing Potato Foam, or Potato Fluff as it was known. The concoction was made from dehydrated potatoes, chilled, flavoured, and doused with raspberry syrup. Stanley never did divulge the complete secret of his *ersatz* ice-cream, which gladdened the hearts and taste buds of many. However, the appearance of fluffy white foam on a cone brought the Man from the Ministry swooping down upon the

Frith establishment, officially to discuss the selling of ice-cream during wartime restrictions. But people were being urged to eat more potatoes — dig for Victory, and all that — so the clever invention was allowed to continue. As one thankful consumer described it, "Pure nectar on a hot summer's day."

Pauline and her sisters, Hazel and Brenda, were popular at school. Children vied to be invited to their birthday parties, for there was always a huge ice-cream birthday cake.

The children's pet mongrel, Jimmy, loved playing out with them in nearby Ravensknowle Park. There were so many nooks and crannies to play hide and seek in, and dens to contrive in the shrubs, before they were removed and the paddling pool made.

People didn't venture far afield in those austere years of petrol rationing. Few had cars in any case. A trip to the park for those not living within walking distance, as the Frith girls did, was a Big Outing. Mr Byewater's café provided refreshments for those who didn't take their own picnics. Children took skipping ropes, a cricket bat and ball, or tennis racquets to while away the happy hours. Peacocks strutting importantly round added an exotic aura to the park, and there was always the museum to wander round if it rained, crammed full of stuffed animals and birds in glass cages, stamps, old coins, butterflies — all with descriptions. And there was a section of Victorian toys, to say nothing of the enormous horse, sliced in half, showing its ribs on one side and a more normal-looking kind of horse when you walked round the other side.

167

Mrs Hirst, a tailoress who lived down Birkhouse in the late 1940s, produced tailor-made coats for the Frith girls at Whitsuntide. Hazel and Brenda had matching coats as they were so close in age they almost could pass as twins. How smart older sister Pauline was, in her brown tweed with velvet pocket flaps and velvet collar. Coats lasted all year round, but when it was proper summer weather, they were discarded and pretty dresses were worn instead.

Miss Tiffany, the Moldgreen haberdasher, owned the little shop where Mrs Frith took her daughters for Whitsuntide bonnets or panamas. How delightful those straw bonnets were, edged with artificial rosebuds or other flowers, with long loose loops of ribbon beneath the chin.

In Brook Street, near the church, was a lady who hired out fancy costumes. At one Ravensknowle Gala Pauline and Hazel were dressed as Jack and Jill, and Brenda dressed as Mary, Mary, Quite Contrary.

The Frith family had a piano (did they play the ditty *Oh, Oh, Antonio, with his ice-cream cart*, one wonders?). Mr Hirst used to tune it. How Pauline loved it when he came round, for he had the enviable talent of being able to "wiggle a tooth, he could even make it disappear at will". Pauline stood by the piano, transfixed by that most unusual of men.

Mr and Mrs Frith were one of the first to own a telephone in the district. Customers used to ask if they may use it in emergencies, leaving 2*d* on the table when the call was finished.

It was a busy, happy childhood, despite there being a war on for most of it. There were wide open spaces to play in, and fields and hedgerows gave freely of their bounty, with blackberries galore to gather in autumn, and bilberries earlier on. For some reason blackberries seemed to be especially fat and luscious when growing in graveyards. When Pauline returned home with a purple mouth her mother wanted to know if she'd eaten them when they should be rinsed first. "Oh no," replied her daughter. "Purple mouth telling lies," retorted Mrs Frith.

A favourite midday dinner was a huge plateful of mashed potato and turnips. Breakfast was usually porridge, but on Sundays they enjoyed bacon, eggs, mushrooms, kidneys (if there were any) and fried cheese. Breakfast-in-a-hurry was dripping on bread. "Bread and scratchit" was the name for bread with margarine applied only thinly, because of rationing, not any shortage of money.

Sunday teatimes seldom varied if there had been enough "points" to hand over to the grocer for a tin of salmon, with a few lettuce leaves. And tinned peaches if there were any, with Carnation milk — or the free bilberries or blackberries — and, best of all, a delicious sherry trifle, which *must* be made, Pauline decreed, in a glass dish so she could see all the different layers: sponge cake with raspberry jam, soaked in sherry; a pretty green, yellow or red jelly; custard, and finally cream scattered with "hundreds and thousands", the tiny coloured confections that made all the difference to what Pauline considered "a real trifle".

In 1942 the family had indulged in a bottle of port, and quite an amount was left in the bottle. Two-year-old Pauline trotted downstairs when the rest of the family were asleep and, seeing the bottle, decided to have a sip. She liked it, and drank some more, then drained the bottle. Next morning her mother was flabbergasted to find her fast asleep on the table. At Dalton nursery next day Mrs Frith was told by one of the assistants in a puzzled tone of voice, "I don't know what's the matter with your Pauline, she's been fast asleep all day."

Winters were so bitterly cold, especially if you lived in a house with high ceilings, that Pauline used to grab her school clothes and put them in bed to try and take the chill off them before hastily putting them on. She used the tepid water from the hot-water bottle for washing her face and hands in preference to the stone-cold water in the tap. Those houses with only a coal fire to heat them — and shortages of coal during the war — often meant that people huddled over the fire, blotches appearing on the front of their legs while their backs were always freezing.

Not long after the war Wilfred Pickles appeared as Buttons at Huddersfield Theatre Royal. He called for a child to join him on stage. Pauline was quick off the mark. She can't recall doing or saying much, but Wilfred ordered, "Give her the money Mabel!" and Pauline returned to her seat 6d better off.

In 1946 an intruder cornered Mr Frith in his shop, and walloped him over the head with a steel pipe. As a result, the ice-cream maker became blind. Thereafter, he never went with his family on seaside holidays again. Instead of having dad to help carry suitcases, Mrs Frith relied on tipping railway porters when going to Blackpool or New Brighton. When there, a pram could be hired for the holiday duration to push the baby, Brenda, around in.

It was difficult in wartime providing toys. But Stanley Frith, before being blinded, made a "marble shoot" for his little daughter Pauline, and someone else made three pandas in a furry material — the big one for Pauline, a not as big one for Hazel, and the smallest for Brenda. At least such toys were unique in those days.

Clean second-hand books were often given to families with children. Money in wartime wasn't as much of a problem as the availability of goods. After the war the girls always received plenty of books and annuals at Christmas. *Girls' Own* Annual, *Beano*, and other popular ones. One year they had a craze for roller skates with noisy metal wheels. Sunday School prizes were always books.

Friday evenings were taken up with Girl Guide meetings, the Moldgreen 28th at Christ Church. In 1956 Pauline Frith was presented with the Queen's Guide Award, the youngest girl ever to attain such an honour in Huddersfield. The Guides went camping all over the place, including Bretton and Eastbourne. Then there was dancing class. Pamela Strickland had a School of Dancing in Moldgreen Congregational Church. Pauline attended on Saturday mornings.

In the early years of his ice-cream business Stanley Frith toured the district with a cart. In 1955 he bought a van. He never wanted to learn Braille, but, as with most blind people, he developed a great sense of touch, and was never without his penknife. When the family went to pantomimes at the Theatre Royal they sat in the balcony, which had brass railings round it. Every year, while the others watched the antics on stage, Stanley brought out his penknife and tightened the screws in the railings, to Pauline's mortification.

Pauline first attended Moldgreen Council School then Dalton, later passing the 11-plus to go to Greenhead High School, by which time the novelty of Frith's Potato Fluff, or Foam, was rapidly becoming a curio of the past.

CHAPTER
TWENTY-FOUR

Joan

Those children who knew nothing but wartime conditions may have been deprived of luxuries such as oranges and bananas, and myriad shop-bought toys, but they certainly gained in many other ways. There's nothing like a community "with its back to the wall" for bringing out that renowned Bulldog Spirit. A spirit of defiance that supersedes all transitory articles that money can buy. Neighbours facing common enemies, poverty, shortages, and later, fathers away from home on active service, tend to become allies for evermore.

Joan Hill went with her brother Geoffrey, and parents Tom and Nellie, to Riddings Rise, Sheepridge, on 6 March 1938. Her first memory is of her dad being wakened for early turn at ICI by Mrs Roper, the "knocker-up". She used an old boot tied to a clothes prop for her job, her strident voice shattering dreams. "Up, Tom, come on, get up", as the boot tapped the bedroom window. The Hill family hadn't an alarm clock, so they paid perhaps 4d a week to Mrs Roper to waken the bread-winners from their slumbers.

For all their lack of material wealth, a code of manners existed, and had to be strictly adhered to.

Children were never allowed to address grown-ups by first names. It had to be a deferential "Mr" or "Mrs", unless familiarity with the family was condoned by the parents. Then "Auntie" and "Uncle" was a compliment to those adults who were regular friends and confidantes of Tom and Nellie. Joan had a healthy respect for "doing the right thing" and "being a good girl", for if she wasn't, she knew who would chastise her — the Bogey Man.

Mrs Hill frequently warned her, "Be a good girl or the Bogey Man will come for you!", which necessitated the landing light being left on at bedtime, until Joan was fast asleep, where no Bogey Man could ever catch her.

Chickens have a habit of coming home to roost, however. The only non-white men children saw in those days were the occasional Asian market traders, going round with a suitcase knocking on doors selling odds and ends. But one beautiful afternoon in the summer holidays Mrs Hill decided to take Joan and Geoffrey to Beaumont Park, which entailed going on a bus into town, then on another up to Crosland Moor. Up the bus step clambered Joan. Then she came to an abrupt halt, turning round in blind terror and trying to push her way back onto the pavement.

"Bogey Man, Bogey Man," the child screamed, catching her breath in terrified sobs. Mrs Hill was totally embarrassed. They had to allow that particular bus to continue without them until the little group on the pavement regained its composure. He was the first black man the child had ever seen.

But even the threat of the dreaded Bogey Man couldn't make Joan desist from sneaking into the pantry and dipping a finger into the tin containing dried egg powder. It made lovely scrambled eggs, and when chocolates and sweets were virtually unobtainable during the war, anything a bit tasty was worth risking a telling-off for. Pom wartime dried potato that just required hot water adding to make acceptable creamed potatoes hadn't the same enticing flavour.

Rewards were inexpensive but treasured. A balloon or goldfish from the rag and bone man who trawled the district ringing a bell and calling "Rags a bones?" Housewives ran out with what few rags they had in the hope of getting 3*d*, 4*d*, or even a tanner for a big bundle. If a child was playing in the garden he might be given a little windmill on a stick, whose sails whirred round attractively when a breeze blew.

Assembly, prayers and hymns began each day at Deighton Council School, after which headmaster Oliver Smith read out the names of "defaulters" or wrongdoers. Joan never heard the same name called out twice after they'd been dealt with in the headmaster's room. Corporal punishment — a quick sharp crack with the ruler — stopped many a child from straying into a life of crime in later years. The deterrent was very necessary for unruly elements in the school. They knew then that they couldn't get away with whatever they intended doing. Oliver Smith's perfectly justified short shock treatment nipped anarchy in the bud. Many potential wrongdoers must, in later life, have thanked him for his discipline.

A particularly dastardly deed that merited more than one lick of the cane was when Joan and Geoffrey had queued for ages outside Sam Lindley's shop. After they handed over their money and coupons, when sweets were rationed, a couple of lads from a rough family emerged from a snicket and accosted them. "Hand over your sweets!" Threatening attitudes made the children do as they were told, though they went home heartbroken. All that saving up, both of money and coupons, only to have them snatched away before even one of the sweets had been tasted. Their mother, when told what had happened, went down the road hand in hand with her tearful children, and knocked on the culprits' door. But nothing could be done about it. The sweets had already been gobbled up.

However, no-one could steal away the halcyon hours of play and make-believe, not even those mean, rough thieves. The hours when Joan and her friends placed stones in the garden in a square, to make a "house". Dock leaves made excellent pretend cabbage and lettuce. And little girls could dress up as real ladies, with long skirts as in days gone by — like they sometimes saw at the pictures — by tying coat sleeves round their waists at the back. Then the material almost reached the ground, and they could curtsy to the king in them.

They had some marvellous inventive neighbours! One dug a huge area out of his back garden to house his air-raid shelter, so the top was level with the rest of the garden. He made steps to go down into it, and put sods of earth on top to make it resemble the rest of the garden. He put a door on it as well. What a wonderful play house it made!

In winter, both boys and girls only had knee-length socks. One particularly cold winter Joan's knees were red and chapped. "Go upstairs and rub some Vaseline on," her dad suggested. Joan picked up the first tin she saw. It was Fiery Jack. She hadn't bothered to read the label, such was her urgency to soothe her reddened knees. How her dad roared with laughter, though he sympathized, at the sight of his daughter running round as if her legs were on fire!

Sunday mornings were lazy, happy times. The children tumbled into their mother's double bed and snuggled down while she sang songs to them, especially old war songs. One of her favourites was:

There's a long, long trail a-winding
Into the land of my dreams,
Where the nightingales are singing,
And the white moon beams;
There's a long, long night of waiting
Until my dreams all come true,
Till the day when I'll be going down that long,
    long trail with you.

"Sing it again, Mother, sing it again." Joan wanted encore after encore. Another song that vied for a repeat was the more robust *Down at the Old Bull and Bush*, and even little brother Raymond joined in.

Come, come, come and make eyes at me
Down at the Old Bull and Bush.
Come, come, drink some port wine with me,
Down at the Old Bull and Bush.
Hear the little German band,
Just let me hold your hand, dear,
Do, do, come and have a drink or two
Down at the Old Bull and Bush.

Then there was *It's a Long Way to Tipperary*, and many others.

To help make the proverbial ends meet, Mrs Hill helped at Whittaker's fish and chip shop, and also used to clean at the Ritz cinema in town. Unexpected perks came Nellie's way. Every stint brought a number of handkerchiefs which had been dropped in the aisles and under seats, and there were more when there had been a tear-jerker shown. Taken home to Riddings Rise, washed and boiled, then hung on the line outside to dry, meant the Hill family were never short of handkerchiefs. They were kept in a drawer by the side of the fireplace. Umbrellas were another frequent find in the Ritz, as well as the odd coin. Nellie accumulated so many umbrellas she could give some away as presents.

One of the down factors of not having a surplus of cash was having to attend the school clinic dentist, not being able to afford to pay for one of your own choice when teeth needed attention. Joan went with her mother to have a filling or tooth extracted one day. It was the clinic's policy for another child's mother to accompany the young patient upstairs, wrongly surmising that children would co-operate more if their own mother was not there. But Joan cried even more when she had to leave her mother, not being in the least bit pacified when the school nurse snapped, "Your mother will be there when you get back!"

Quite a different matter was being asked to go to "The Wooden Hut", as a local fish and chip shop was known.

Gas wasn't used for cooking, and instead the pans were heated over a wood fire, making the fish and chips taste far better, thought Joan. Gas masks in their brown cases had to be carried everywhere, slung on a cord over the shoulders. But "going to t' chip hole" surely wasn't deemed far enough away to warrant any attack by Jerry.

Lucy Jowett, an elderly lady, not wanting to be seen at the outsales of a public house herself, sometimes asked Joan if she would take a jug to the Woolpack for her. A man wearing a long mackintosh waited until the landlord was out of sight, then flung open his mac before the little girl, who didn't wait for the jug of beer, but flew home. There were some funny people in the world.

Joan thought her dad was wonderful. Once, having cadged an old orange box from a local grocer, he made a doll's pram for her, with old bits of wood for handles. He painted it black, as most prams were black then. No other little girl round about had one like it. Joan treasured it all the more because her dad, her clever dad, had made it himself.

It was a sad day for her when Tom joined the Royal Artillery. Housewives were increasingly taking over what had formerly been work only undertaken by men. They even had a lady coalman, who delivered sacks of coal to their house. Most wives during the war tended the gardens. Tom had an allotment as well.

The council, to encourage householders to keep surroundings neat, ran competitions to find the best estate garden. Of course, with paper shortages, there wasn't much litter. What a pity they couldn't grow oranges and bananas in their gardens! Joan recalls the day they had one orange to be shared between the three children. Their mother carefully peeled it into three segments, telling Joan, Geoffrey and Raymond to suck them slowly, to make them last. It might be a long time before they tasted another. And what a momentous occasion when the children saw what they had heard about, and seen pictures of, but never actually tasted — a couple of bananas when their mother queued at a greengrocer's for them.

Wartime it may have been, but many traditions continued, such as the Whitsuntide walks, and carnivals, with fancy-dress parades in farmer Dan Appleyard's cow field, sack races, three-legged races, and egg and spoon races. There were money prizes, with 6d for the winner, and perhaps a silver threepenny bit for the second. There was all the fun of the fair, and a local girl was chosen as Carnival Queen.

Religion was important in people's lives. A faith in God was often the only "glue" that prevented many sorely tried, war-weary mothers from falling apart.

Trying to provide meals for hungry families out of next to nothing and lack of money had been the worry before the war, then food shortages added to the dilemma. Those with allotments came off best, and were generous enough to give surplus to families with children, and old people too frail to Dig For Victory themselves. Digging for Victory and for each other could well have been the slogan of ordinary, working-class communities. Good old "Winnie" was rightly proud of such good neighbours, who, in their way, helped to win the war.

Simple recipes of vegetables helped families greatly, and few dishes could be tastier than scalloped potatoes, a Ministry of Food idea. Scrub 2 lb of potatoes and cut them into thick slices. Wash a couple of leeks and cut finely. Mix together a heaped tablespoonful of flour, a teaspoon of salt, and pepper to taste. Put in alternate layers of potatoes and leeks, sprinkling each layer with seasoned flour, the top layer being potatoes. Pour in three teacups full of hot milk, then bake for an hour in a moderate oven. There was enough for four or five people, and cost nothing but the gas or electricity if you grew your own vegetables.

Those not working used to get together for the weekly Bright Hour in the Sunday school on Tuesday afternoons, for a few hymns, a chat, a speaker, a cup of tea and biscuits (if available), and moral support in difficult times. Members of the Bright Hour organized a trip to the Yorkshire Dales, and someone had a camera — *and* a film. Even films were hard to come by during the war. Chapel stalwarts Harold Charlesworth and Harry Gibson accompanied the party, which included a number from Riddings Rise, including Sally Briggs, Maureen Briggs, Mrs Clelland, and daughters Jean and Pat. An outing meant looking one's best. It just wouldn't do to be seen in public without wearing hat, coat and gloves. Strings of "pearls" and brooches added to the dressed-up feeling and the enjoyment of any excursion.

Huddersfield Market Hall had a stall where lovely straw bonnets and hats were sold. Joan's mother bought one from there every Whitsuntide. Inexpensive outfits could be bought at Henry's, on New Street. In the "top notch", rather too expensive for Mrs. Hill's little brood, was Kaye's down King Street. Joan, after longingly gazing at pretty dresses, coats and hats in Kaye's window asked her mother, "Can't I have something from there?" "We're going to the market," was the reply.

Joan had a celluloid baby doll. Every now and again its forehead became squashed in, either by rough play or accident. The way to restore it was to put the doll in a warm place, where gradually the fault was restored.

When Joan's brother Raymond was a baby, she named another doll after him. It had a pot head and pot legs, with a cloth body. Joan thought the world of it. Alas, its head was broken one day. Mrs Hill promised to take "Raymond" to the Dolls' Hospital on Shambles Lane. Days, weeks went by.

"Isn't Raymond better yet?" its little owner kept asking. But Raymond the doll never did return home to

Riddings Rise. His illness was terminal. Mrs Hill couldn't afford to pay for the doll doctor's services.

"I've been to see them love, and they can't mend your doll. It was too poorly to be made better."

Those words were etched on Joan's mind for a long time. "Raymond" would be sold to another child whose mother could afford to buy it, and the poor doll would have to learn to live with a different name and owner. The physical presence of a doll may be taken away, but the memories live on forever.

Turning one's thoughts to Christmas never failed to raise spirits. Before Tom joined the army he used to hang one of his socks over the mantelpiece on Christmas Eve, writing a note to himself, which was supposed to be from Father Christmas. "Sorry, no presents for big boys." And the sock was stuffed with cold cinders from the fire.

Mrs Hill had no trouble persuading the children to go to bed, for they knew that the sooner bedtime came, the sooner "He" would come. Though sleep didn't come straightaway. How could it, when Geoffrey kept urging his sister to "have a look at the bottom of the bed".

When they were little, Geoffrey, Joan and Raymond slept in the same bed, with Joan in the middle, all wearing cosy winceyette striped pyjamas that had been put in the side oven to warm before being snuggled into.

A few days prior to Christmas one year during the war, a big box arrived at the house. Nellie warned the excited youngsters, "It must not be opened yet, it's a secret."

Their Aunt Emma worked at ICI on Leeds Road. On the opposite side was a prisoner-of-war camp. Children, including the three Hill youngsters, used to taunt the men when they exercised in the yard, which was surrounded by barbed wire. The prisoners lived in wooden huts, and the initials POW were printed on the sleeves of their uniforms. To occupy themselves, the prisoners were invited to make toys. Auntie Emma did as Tom suggested, and asked the prisoners to make a blackboard and easel for Joan. On it, Tom had chalked "Merry Xmas Joan. Love, Daddy." There was a wooden, two-storey doll's house as well, and a wooden pull-along cart, all made by the prisoners of war, quite unknown to the children. Tom had managed to get *Dandy* and *Beano* annuals as well, and some monkey nuts.

Every now and again the doll's house doubled as a hospital. Geoff's tin soldiers, the ones with heads broken off, went into the "hospital", where a major operation took place. A matchstick was plunged into each body and the head reunited with it.

Joan was faced with an awful problem one Christmas. Schoolfriends insisted, "There isn't a Father Christmas, it's your dad." She didn't want to believe them. But on the night of Christmas Eve she wakened when she heard a noise in the bedroom — and saw her dad with his arms full of parcels. Next morning, reluctantly, she confronted him. "There isn't a Father Christmas is there, Dad? It's you."

184

Tom Hill's face was the picture of injured innocence and dismay, "Well, if you don't believe there *is* a Father Christmas, you don't get presents." And *he* believed in him. Joan's mind was in utter confusion. She must have dreamt about seeing him, because of what she'd been told by her silly friends. Oh, poor dad. Joan was worried stiff. How could she tell him there was no Father Christmas? But who was it then?

When she was older, she had to be in by a certain time, not a minute later. But if she showed up earlier, the question was, "You're early — what have you been up to?"

During his service with the Royal Artillery, Tom was in Cairo. He didn't get home again until 1946, missing the VE Day street party on 8th May so enjoyed by those still at home on Riddings Rise.

About that time Joan came across one of the best inventions ever, in her opinion. Joan was left-handed, and her mother maintained Joan cut loaves in a lop-sided manner. Now there was a sliced loaf, all ready cut. But after buying one the novelty wore off, and Mrs Hill continued baking her own bread. It was cheaper, and better, too.

A feast far more stupendous that any sliced loaf was on the horizon though — that Riddings Rise street party. How mothers rose to the challenge! They went round knocking on every door to suggest everyone contributed food to celebrate the end of the dreary war, to celebrate victory, and, maybe, to look forward to a future which was better than they had had for their children. All were united in their desire to give the children something really wonderful to remember.

How busy they were! How joyful. Bubbling over with enthusiasm and ideas, putting up bunting and flags, and everything they could lay their hands on that was red, white and blue.

As they made sandwiches that morning of 8 May 1945, they prayed that it would keep fine. Tables were dragged out of houses and laid out down the middle of the street. Someone brought out a piano. Mrs Briggs, Mrs McNamara, Mrs McDonald, all of them, worked with a zest never before equalled.

In the afternoon there were games and the singing of war songs filled the air with a euphoria that was infectious. Even the dogs and cats wore red, white and blue ribbons and jumped about wondering what was happening down Riddings Rise.

Chairs were drawn up to the tables, sandwiches appeared at intervals down the long length, as well as buns, biscuits, jellies and a big, wobbly pink blancmange. Then some of the helpers went across to Joe Taylor's shop to collect the *pièce de resistance* — an absolutely enormous sponge cake, beautifully decorated in patriotic colours, with "VE Day" piped across the top. It was carried still in the tin so it wouldn't break. Nothing must happen to spoil the glorious day.

What a party! What a sing song to end all sing songs! How they Rolled Out the Barrel, Hung Out the Washing on the Siegfried Line, and sang *A Nightingale Sang In Berkeley Square*, and if there was no nightingale in Riddings Rise, at least scores of enthusiastic songsters just couldn't stop singing. Toddlers too young to know what all the celebrations were about caught the mood and behaved impeccably — maybe because they had never seen such bounty on a table before.

On and on they went, everybody taking up the song started by someone at the tables. *There'll be Blue Birds Over the White Cliffs of Dover, Bless 'em All, There'll Always be an England, When They Sound the Last All Clear, I'm Going to Get Lit Up (When the Lights Go On in London), Kiss Me Goodnight, Sergeant Major* and *We'll Meet Again*.

Most poignant of all the war songs was the one broadcast in France by Gracie Fields — *Good night, Children, Everywhere*. With a tender thought to all evacuated children. This was the chorus:

Good night, children, everywhere.
Your mummy thinks of you tonight.
Lay your head upon your pillow,
Don't be a kid or a weeping willow,
Close your eyes and say a prayer,
And surely you can find a kiss to spare.
Tho' you are far away she's with you night and
day,
Good night, children everywhere.

The fine weather held until tea was finished, then rain sent the merrymakers across to the YMCA, next to Edmondson's, the plumber's shop, where singing and games continued. Never had so much red, white and blue been seen together all at once.

Joan wore a blue dress with red collar and red sleeves. Her plaits were tied with white ribbons. Everybody had been asked to dress in patriotic colours if possible.

Someone had managed to get a film, and the Riddings Rise VE Day street party was captured for all time. Josephine Calverly holding her little brother in her arms, Hazel Briggs, Eileen Calverly, Sheila McDonald, Margaret McNamara, Sheila McNamara, Rita Parkin and Elaine Parkin, Jacqueline Hardcastle and her sister, Peter Tighe, Derek Woodhouse, Roy Hepworth, Jack Beckett, Maureen Briggs, Margaret Walker, Mary Bagshaw. All were united in having survived the war years — and childhood — in a strong, warm-hearted community.

When blackout curtains were no longer required for their original purpose, it was suggested that another "Get Together" would be a good idea — a concert in one of the back gardens, given by residents of "the Rise". Mrs McNamara went round again, alerting everybody, telling them the date, time and to "be there".

Mrs Clelland, good with a needle, set to work measuring participants for costumes. Many fittings took place in the Clelland household for skirts created from people's old blackout curtains, with jazzy coloured braid to liven them up. There couldn't have been more excitement if the concert was to take place in the Albert Hall, never mind a back garden down

Riddings Rise. What talents were fostered when children were encouraged to put on concerts in their own "back yards".

Then in 1948 a show was promoted by Deighton Sunday school. It was called "The Fairy Chain". Yet again Mrs Clelland's talents as a seamstress were called upon, to make the costumes. It was a pleasure, not a toil, to see the fruits of one's labours in all their splendour on stage. Sunday school teachers Miss Blanche Chinn and Mrs Oldroyd "coached" the youngsters in dialogue, song and dance. Children who took part were Maureen Briggs, Doreen Plowman, Betty Garner (the Prince), Jean Clelland (Princess), Pat Birmingham, Muriel Briggs, Christine Robson, Joan Hill and others.

How sad that Days of Childhood and Make Believe pass so swiftly by. Even in wartime, childhood has a magical, ethereal quality about it. It is a never-never land where, despite poverty, material deprivations, and dreams that all too often fail to come true, bluebells, buttercups and daisies continue to flourish, and to gladden the hearts of children everywhere.

There is a long, long trail a-winding, where we can all turn back the pages, and take that long, long trail again — winding it back to our own childhood.